Journey of the Awakened Heart

The author of this book does not dispense medical advice or prescribe the use of any technique as treatment for physical or medical problems without the advice of a physician, either directly or indirectly. The intent of the author is to offer information of a general nature to help you in your quest for enhanced wellbeing. In the event you use any of the information in this book for yourself (which is your constitutional right), the author and the publisher assume no responsibility for your actions.

Edited by Stephanie Gunning
Cover design by Maryam Movsumov

ISBN: 0-9831433-0-7
ISBN-13: 978-0-9831433-0-7

Journey of the Awakened Heart

Discovering Who You Are
and Why You Are Here
The Teachings of Archangel Michael

Jeff Fasano

The Angel News Network
New York, N.Y. - Los Angeles, California 2010

To my mom, Margaret Fasano, and my dad,
Thomas Fasano, my greatest teachers and my best
friends.
To my brother, Tommy;
we made it through together.

Contents

Preface

Journey of the Awakened Heart is a book about living our soul purpose. The teachings came through me from a divine source that emanates from a fifth dimensional realm known as the Archangelic Realm of Michael. It is a high vibrational energy that raises our resonance and vibration to the vibration of love and joy. The teachings seek to move us from our mind to our heart so that we may develop self-love in order to connect with our passion and purpose in this lifetime.

For some of us, there is a gap between how we're living and how we say we want to live. Once living soul-purposefully, this gap disappears. Your soul purpose will be organically revealed to you as you work sequentially through the various messages and processes of this book. After you clear your blocks to self-love, you reflect upon your talents and gifts, gradually coming to understand the fullness of who you are and what you want, because "you cannot get to point X," as Michael says, "without first going through points A, B, and C."

In looking back, you could say this is exactly the same way that I became a trance channel: through organic revelation. It wasn't something I set out to do consciously; it was a byproduct of my personal healing process.

"I dare you to go to my healer, Robert Baker," my now-good friend Alexandra Boos, a fashion model whom I had met at a photo shoot I was doing only a week earlier, said to me. The stars were aligned because it was my good friend Maria Rangel who brought Alexandra and I together.

A few months earlier, I'd been on a photo shoot in Riverside Park overlooking the Hudson River from Manhattan. West 84th Street being a street with phenomenal old buildings on it, including the house where Edgar Allen Poe once lived, my model and I moved down the block from Riverside towards West End looking for interesting facades. We were in a doorway shooting pictures when a slender man with curly blond hair and wire-rimmed glasses opened the front door and looked at us for a moment, and then went back inside. That man was Robert.

Jump forward again to the day Alexandra captured my attention. I was up on a chair aiming my camera down towards a model when Alex walked into the room. I'd met her once before and there was nothing magical about our connection. But on this occasion, as she walked through the doorway and I glanced at her, my knees buckled and I saw a flash of blue light shoot across the room from her solar plexus to mine. That's the area of the third chakra, an energy center in the body that is related to our purpose in life.

Whatever you may believe about trance channels, I'm probably not what you're imagining. I don't see spiritual light normally. I can't see auras. As much as I've tried, doing so has never been within my capabilities—

except for that once. I knew seeing the blue light was meaningful and that Alex was someone significant to me.

A couple of days later, Alex challenged me, "I dare you to see him." I called Robert. We made an appointment. A few more days after that I walked from my apartment a few blocks further north down Broadway to West 84th Street, arrived at the building where Robert lived, he answered the door, I walked inside, and I said, "I know you." I told him the story I told you about him opening the door, and then he sat me down and we started talking. He said, "I want to lay out the parameters of the healing work we'll do," and explained that it was a six-month commitment and what it entailed. He looked at me and said, "So how are you feeling about that? Do you need anything from me right now?"

I replied, "I am in. I am in forever. I am doing this." Well, I might not have said it aloud. But I felt my heart opening up to Robert and I felt so much love in that moment. I knew I needed to work with him, that's what I needed right then.

Once before I had done therapy, which lasted for the allotted length of time that the insurance policy at my job would cover. Not once did I feel a soul or heart connection with the man who was my therapist. And his sessions never did a thing for me. I liked my therapist, I liked having someone to talk to, but it didn't feel the same as doing therapy with Robert. I had known that something was missing in my life. And I knew that I needed someone who would get me. Robert was the guy.

It was 2000, the turn of the millennium. The kind of healing work Robert does is bioenergetic therapy. Our focus at that time was on clearing old patterns of wounding that came from childhood and my family of origin so I could begin to know who I am and learn to love myself. As each defensive layer of energy, thoughts, and feelings was peeled off, the process raised my vibration and opened me up to higher levels of consciousness.

That's what Michael's work does, too. It helps us learn to be able to access higher states. Life is much more harmonious when lived from higher energy states.

In addition to being a tremendously gifted therapist, Robert Baker has another gift. He is a trance channel for the Archangel Gabriel. He also co-founded Children of Light with his business partner Ron Baker, a spiritual group in New York City. Once a week they would hold a meditation session for a group of committed spiritual seekers. After six weeks of counseling with him, I attended my first Gabriel channeling. Trance channeling is where a person relinquishes his or her connection to the third dimension and to the physical body (he or she goes to sleep, so to speak), while an outside higher vibration energy enters the body and uses the voice of the channel to connect with those who are listening. This is also how the messages in this book came to us.

I still remember the first time I went and sat there in the circle and heard Gabriel's message. It was so real to me. I never questioned the reality of Gabriel. I knew that the voice speaking was not Robert and that it was another energy coming through his body. I closed my eyes and listened to the words Gabriel was saying, and also felt the message delivered in my body energetically. It was real, loving, and compassionate.

Alexandra and some of the other people who were just joining the meditation group at the same time were a little bit skeptical. Alex asked me, "Don't you ever question it?"

I responded, "No, it is as real to me as the big toe on my left foot."

The work I was doing with Robert was an evolutionary progression of making a commitment to recognizing who I am with all my talents and gifts, and learning to love myself and live my purpose. Robert helped my career as a photographer grow. I hadn't been a photographer for long, so I was learning to live the life I said I wanted. It was an intense and joyous time as I created a life that was more productive and rewarding.

The first time I channeled was on the day of my forty-fourth birthday. Most of the people in our spiritual community had gone to Peru on a spiritual pilgrimage with Children of Light led by Robert and Ron. Even though I wanted to go on that trip, I was not feeling this one. So I stayed behind in New York. In celebration of my birthday, I went for a session with a healing practitioner named Debbra Gill, who is a friend of mine. Because it was my birthday, I had been compiling a list on a legal pad of what I wanted to release from my life. She told me, "Bring it." I tore the piece of paper off the pad and folded up my list, and when I arrived for my healing session, we put the folded up piece of paper on Debbra's altar. We never opened it or looked at it. I just took my shoes off and hopped up onto her massage table fully clothed. Debbra's works with the energy of different crystals. She strategically placed crystals on different points on my body, including my upturned hands. I closed my eyes and she started her work.

As I was laying there, I silently thought, "Release and let go. Release and let go. Release and let go." I repeated it three times—and then I did.

Letting go was cool. I felt myself going somewhere else and knew I wasn't there on the table anymore. And I was surrounded by all sorts of warriors. As a photographer, I am a visual person, and I need to see what is going on, which, I believe, is why my healing experience was so visual that day. One warrior would pop up and then he would vanish. Another warrior would pop up and vanish. It went on and on. The warriors wore different garb, and I knew they were warriors I had been or known from different lifetimes.

What I had wanted to release was my armor. That day, I wanted to let go of everything that armored my heart. I knew this, but I didn't write it down on the paper exactly like that. The warriors came up because they were the energy I used to fend off love and to keep me from opening my heart and being seen for who I am. They stood in the way of being loved really and truly for who I am.

As soon as the warriors would be shown to me, they would vanish into thin air. But there was one I called a Zulu warrior, who wouldn't leave. His energy was healed and he was released later on a trip to Burma. But that day he didn't vanish. He stubbornly remained.

That was when I looked up and realized that, wherever I was, I wasn't lying on the table. I had left my body. It felt as if was up in a corner of the room watching what was transpiring though I wasn't actually seeing anything. All of a sudden everything went dark. Then, I opened my eyes and found myself looking up at Debbra and I remember saying. "That was a short hour."

Her response was, "What? That was two hours—and while you were gone you channeled the Archangel Michael!"

I looked at her and knew it to be true. "Yeah, I know," I said. Although I didn't know what Michael said or what happened while I was out of my body, in my heart and soul I knew it to be true. Channeling was an aspect of the divine plan of my soul.

It was amazing!

Debbra had experienced channeling previously, and so she asked many pertinent questions: "Who are you? Why Jeff? How did you get here?" One thing Michael told her was, "Gabriel brought us to you." It makes perfect sense, because according to research I've done since then, Gabriel and Michael are the two archangels that have the most interaction with humans. They were with Jesus, and Michael is Jesus' messenger.

In case you might be feeling a bit impressed with all of this, there's something that must be said, which is this: even though I channel the energy of Michael, I am no better or worse than anyone else. It doesn't matter any more that I have this gift than you have your gifts.

We are all equal beings on this planet. This is why I can walk through the streets of a city in Cuba or a village in Burma and feel akin to the people there. In my heart, I recognize that I am one with them, and they are one with me. I feel for people. Watching the news about the earthquake in Haiti in 2009 or the devastation of hurricane Sandy in the U.S. in 2012 and seeing images of the destruction and pain, I felt connected to the people of those regions, as if their losses were my losses.

Everybody is relevant. No matter who you are and where you come from, you are relevant. You are here at this time in a body on earth for an important reason. Everybody has gifts and talents. These are diverse. But we are one. Everyone is lovable. Everybody matters. Everyone has an important life purpose, a reason for being. The purpose of this book is to guide and support you in realizing yours, in understanding your gifts and talents, and knowing why you matter so very much just for being you.

We need each other if we are to succeed in our evolution. No more can we go it alone and hope for the best. Rather we grow mutually and collectively. I honor those of my companions who have helped me understand my value and embrace my purpose.

The next step I took was with the assistance of my friend Brian Brennan, who was another member of Robert's weekly meditation group. Everybody else we knew from the group was on the trip to Peru, but, like me, Brian had stayed home. He was the perfect person to offer me support. After leaving Debbra's apartment, I phoned Brian and told him, "I channeled!" I explained the whole scene to him and, frankly, I was freaking out. He was great. He said, "Calm down. What do you need?"

I love that question. It's always a good one to ask when you're feeling emotionally overwhelmed. For a couple of weeks, I phoned Brian almost every single day because I was freaking out and I needed someone to talk to about it. I knew what happened was real. But I never asked, "Why me?" I was just freaking out. There are things in life that don't require an explanation. Our feelings are one of them. That question is a good response when you or someone you know is having an intense feeling.

First, Brian asked me a few questions, and then he asked, "Do you want to bring in the energy again?" Oh yeah!

Debbra, Brian, and I met at a friend's apartment and we did it. I sat on the sofa, closed my eyes, and mentally repeated the same thing I had on Debbra's table: "I release and let go." To this day, that's exactly what I do to go into a trance every time I channel. But since then I have added, "This is not about me." I say everything three times. As soon as I thought those words, I saw a flash of white light and then I saw a vision of Michael, wings stretched open behind him, walking, holding a scepter. The ancient Egyptian God of light, Horus, who has the head of a falcon, was walking next to him on his right. And there was an eagle flying above them. When I opened my eyes, Brian and Debbra were both watching me, saying, "Thanks, Jeff." Michael had given them personal messages.

When I begin to channel, it is like I am watching a movie. Over the years, the vision I see has changed shape, as I have grown and my frequency is higher. Now my typical vision looks like a hologram, a transparent image of Michael on a white horse with a scepter in his hand. I see this outline of Michael and his wings and the scepter, and he points the scepter towards me as we begin. The next thing I know it's done.

The longest amount of time I have ever channeled in one session is between three and four hours. But it always seems as if it is an instant to me. When I open my eyes, I can see that everything I thought was real and three-dimensional is different than before. My heart is open so much to people around me that my purpose always is fully revealed to me in those moments. I know why I am here and what I am here to do.

How, Why, and from Where the Teachings of Michael Come to Us

Since the gift of trance channeling was revealed to me in 2002, I have been a messenger for this non-physical energy known as Archangel Michael. Michael comes through me with powerful messages of guidance and support for all those who are on a personal path of self-mastery and moving towards fully realized lives of world service. He imparts wisdom, guidance, and support so we can move into the depth of our heart to know who we are and reveal our talents and gifts. Also, so we can understand why we are here and move forward together in service for the greater good of the world and our planet.

In 2007, five individuals came together to listen to a message from Michael. As part of this message, which I transcribed and entitled "The Five Aspects," Michael gave us an exercise that led us to identify the five most important aspects of our lives at that time. It had such a profound affect on us individually that we decided to gather again at a later date and learn more. What we didn't know was that Michael was leading us to form a group. When we gathered again, he introduced us to five agreements that would become the defining intention of this new group.

The Five Agreements were given to us as principles to embody and use as guidelines in how we are living our lives. Michael has explained that embodying them "represents a commitment of moving from 'Me-consciousness' to 'We-consciousness' and towards awakening the truth within your heart." Our group continued to gather every week for almost a full year after that, and Michael, through the messages and exercises he gave us during this period, led us to understand how we could begin to realize our commitment. The Five Agreements are designed to raise the level of consciousness, resonance, and vibration of the world by bringing people together in harmony with all those who are committed to creating unity and equality.

Soon we began inviting others to join us at our gatherings and Michael led us through the process you are holding in your hands. It was in these gatherings that Part One, "Who Are You?" and Part Two, "Why Are You Here?" came to us in longer versions. I knew in my heart how important the teachings of Michael are and that they needed to be shared with the world, so I was willing to contribute my presence and serve as a channel.

Michael's words have changed my life and they can change your life, too. If you have come to a point where the old way is no longer working for you and you need to change to go further, you can make that decision now.

The members of the soul family present when the original channeled messages occurred appeared one by one in my life. Brian was the first. Peter Frame was the second. In 2001, I had gone on a trip to Egypt led by Robert. In the first meeting for the tour, Robert gave us a partner exercise to do. We were supposed to work with someone we didn't know. Peter turned to me and asked, "Jeff would you like to pair with me?" It was an exercise where we took turns asking and responding to the question, "What do you need?" (My favorite question.) I am so grateful to Peter for bringing me out of my shell.

Later, in a temple dedicated to the lion-headed sun goddess Sekhmet, I went up to Peter when he was crying and put my hand on his back. That was the first time I felt I was an energy healer. He helped me know who I am.

Philip Collins came into my life, but not right at the beginning of my channeling. He came later and we exchanged healing sessions. "You could be an influential healer in your lifetime," he said. "I see that in you based on channeling Michael. There is only one person standing in the way, you. I want to work with you. I see what you could be." In our sessions, Philip helped me release my attachment both to being Jeff the photographer and to being Jeff the channel. He helped me realize that photography and channeling were merely gifts and talents, rather than the essence of who I am.

"Just be Jeff because that's who I love," he told me. Philip is a tremendous coach. He had a massively successful career in which he used to work with George Lucas, the creator of Star Wars and Raiders of the Lost Arc, and before that he also worked with photographers like Diane Arbus and Richard Avedon. He helped me put together a viable plan for advancing my photography career and my life.

The contribution of my friend and colleague Joel Anastasi was not revealed to me immediately; although I always had faith he would play a significant role in how my soul plan unfolded. In winter 2010, I traveled to Florida and co-led a workshop based on the teachings of Michael. A brilliant journalist and author of a book, The Second Coming, on the teaching of Archangel Gabriel as channeled by Robert Baker, he adapted Michael's processes and produced a powerful transformative book entitled Life Mastery. He shared this in the workshop, and I finally had the opportunity to be present and conscious while he taught the material that I normally channel while in trance.

Joel helped me to develop a sense of self—and to develop an understanding of my purpose. And that was essential, for honestly I could not have gotten here on my own.

Another individual came into my life and helped me realize my soul purpose, and I would like to acknowledge her for her role in the writing and creation of

Journey of the Awakened Heart. Her name is Stephanie Gunning. Ultimately I asked my good friend Stephanie, an author, editor, and publishing consultant, to help me shape Michael's words into the form you see right now. I cannot imagine anyone better suited to the task because she has known me since the days of the Gabriel group and is also a spiritual healer.

Michael's energy is not the only energy I have channeled over the years. In addition to Michael, I have channeled the energy of Jeshua, Raphael, Mary, and others. And, in the process, I have learned to be intentional about whose energy I am bringing in. I have grown up. This means I am responsible for my life. I recognize that I am the creator of my life; nobody else is responsible for me—not my mom and not my dad, not my friends, not my coworkers.

Being grown up means that after you get up in the morning, as you go to brush your teeth and look into your eyes, the person you see reflected in the mirror is the true you. It is not the mask anymore. You don't have to portray what other people want you to portray, and you don't have to live the life they want you to live. As an adult human being, you are in charge of your life—making your choices, setting your boundaries, and stating your needs—and, because you fully know your essence (aka who you are), you love you. And based upon that tremendous love for self, you realize your talents and gifts. Based upon that, you see there is a greater purpose for why you are alive.

My purpose is continuously evolving and it has many facets to it—so will yours. I remind myself constantly who I am by reviewing my life and my accomplishments. What really defines me…the thing that gives me the greatest satisfaction outside of my own creative process is seeing others living their passion, having the lives they say they want, and fully expressing their creativity in life. I feel incredibly excited when I am watching a live theatrical performance on Broadway and the actors are giving their all, or when I'm at a concert listening to musicians who love making music. They're really living their lives as they're doing their work. I love artists and performers.

I also love traveling around the world and meeting people, so that's part of my purpose. Every single teaching and lecture that has moved through me as a channel has been encoded in my DNA, and part of my soul purpose is healing, writing, teaching and being a messenger for Michael's messages. But I love taking pictures and I love being a photographer. It is such an important part of my life that has opened many doors for me on many different levels. Photography opened the door to Michael.

The beauty of the message in this book, and of the teachings of Michael in general, is that it reinforces the shared understanding that we're in a new era of We-consciousness and resonant causation—meaning, once we've released our mental conditioning we can create our lives effortlessly from matching our vibration with the vibration of who and what is around us; we can create from love. Having done the exercises in this book more than once and having spent a good deal of time evaluating and editing them for this book, I know that when my heart feels love I am moving in the right direction. That's where I'll find the people who share my enthusiasm and values. And I hope you're one of them.

Peace
Jeff

Michael Speaks

We welcome you at this wonderful and most glorious time, as you are now ready to emerge into a new life of community, harmony, and equality. Whether or not you know it consciously, you have reached the point where you are ready, open, and available to all that is coming to you and to receive what you say you want. This is not necessarily anything outside of you that validates or gratifies you; it is something that resonates with you. You have previously moved through a healing process that enabled you to know who you are and why you are here. Some who are reading understand fully why you are here, and some of you are just getting a glimpse of it. The important thing is that you are ready to find within you the answer to where you are going out in the world.

As you begin the process of exploration in this book, we begin by asking: why are you here? Are you here to get something for yourself? Are you here to move out in the world to express your gifts and talents? Or are you here just to get by, endure life, and survive? In your heart, you know the answers and it is time to take the next step. You are here for the purpose of world service, and loving who you are and what you do is world service.

We, Michael, are simply a resonance, a vibration at a specific frequency, which emanates from the Archangelic Realm of Michael. We come to you with specific messages that are of this specific frequency. Each person vibrates at a certain level. Those who are attracted within the depth and breadth of their hearts to the frequency of this energy are singularly encoded with it. Thus, the frequency from your heart connects—or resonates—with the frequency of this energy from the Archangelic Realm of Michael. That is why you are attracted to reading, understanding, and feeling the energy of the words in this book.

The essence of this frequency and the message it is carrying are about making a journey from the core of your mind into the core of your heart. The twenty messages and lessons contained within this book are tools to be utilized while making this journey. As you commence reading the first message in Part One, "Who Are You?" you will begin a process of allowing your heart to become the guiding force of your life. For some, the shift in consciousness that makes this possible is gradual. For others, it is sudden. The process involves peeling layer upon layer of wounding from around your heart, until you have moved into the core of your heart and uncovered the essence of you, your truth.

As you release each layer of wounding that surrounds your heart, you will also raise the level of resonance and vibration within you. This is because each layer of wounding is filled with dense, lower-vibration energy, which simply represents what you learned in the past—during childhood and through trauma—about how to survive in the world and how you were conditioned. Peeling away these layers is the intention of this specific frequency and level of energy that emanates from the Archangelic Realm of Michael.

After you have completed the ten exercises in Part One, you will move on to the series of messages and lessons in Part Two, "Why You Are Here?" As you move along the pathway set forth for you, you will discover the talents and gifts you are here to give. The purpose of Part Two is to lead you to cross the threshold of a doorway of consciousness. By engaging in a discovery process, you will raise the level of vibration of the world and help to co-create a new world of harmony, community, and equality.

We, Michael, come as a level of energy of support and guidance for you on your pathway. We simply make suggestions through the wonderful and glorious soul (Jeff Fasano) who has made the choice to be the messenger (the channel) of this energy. This glorious soul is connected to the specific frequency within him that connects with our frequency, which enables him to impart our message. The frequency is consistent; it is the same for all who experience it. As this frequency moves through this messenger, the energy permeates your heart. Then, it is up to you how you choose to interpret it.

What is actually connecting with you—things uniquely yours—are the frequency in your own heart and the ways you utilize your five physical senses to interpret it. As the frequency of the Archangelic Realm of Michael penetrates the depth of your heart, it radiates outward to give you the impetus to commit to the teachings. It does not connect to your mental body whatsoever. It only connects with the frequency of your heart.

Introduction

As we have walked our pathways on the journey of self-mastery we've all been led to, we have read many books that have given us valuable information to think about, and we've been introduced to many spiritual tools to improve our lives. We have stored much of this information in our minds. Now, many of us are wondering, "What's next? What do we do with all of the information?" Our next step is to bring what we have stored in our minds into our hearts, so that we may actually live from it.

The material in this book, Journey of the Awakened Heart, which was created by Michael for the mass awakening of consciousness in the world we are living, is intended to guide us step by step, each at our own personal pace, to move within our heart space. Many have found it life changing.

Lately have you noticed yourself saying?

- I want to move out of the old ways of doing things that seem to get me nowhere."
- "I am in the same old place and still struggling in my life."
- "I want to move into abundance and enjoy my life."

If these words sound familiar—meaning, if ending your struggle, moving into greater abundance, deepening your connections with others, finding fulfillment, and enjoying life is what you truly want, then developing a new approach to living is now of utmost importance. The crux of the matter is this: you have practiced the "old ways" your entire life. You cannot expect to embrace new ways without a similar degree of practice. Contained within these pages, therefore, are messages and lessons that will assist you in discovering a new, highly individual, and self-mastered way of life that is more enjoyable.

Making the commitment to move from the old approach to life into the new approach to life is what makes the transition entirely possible. That commitment you make, however, is to no one and nothing outside of you. It is a choice, pure and simple, to love yourself, express yourself authentically, and pursue only those experiences and activities with which, and the people with whom you resonate. Resonance is a term that describes harmonious vibrations. You are a vibratory being. This book, if it is in harmony with your essence, can facilitate the movement forward toward living the life you say you want, and loving yourself more than you ever have before.

Collectively, those of us for whom this material provided by Michael resonates have come now to a point in the world where we have the ability to make new choices. We can let go of looking outside of ourselves to get something "out there" to fill us up in order to feel validated. We know our deepest satisfaction comes from within us. We now have the capacity to give our unique gifts and talents to the world, and, through the giving, to realize our potential to create a new world of harmony, community, and equality. Yet, the only way this can happen in actuality is to transform within our selves.

As Michael has stated so eloquently on different occasions, those of us for whom this message is intended have come to the intersection of the old way of life and the new. We already know the old way of life doesn't work, and it holds less and less attraction as time goes by for those of us who have been working on ourselves for these many years. But we're also not yet ready to move forward and step onto the path into the unknown because we cannot feel yet the distinction between living a life based upon conditioning and living a life based upon the harmonious energy of resonant causation. Something has to happen here, at this juncture, that prepares us.

Journey of the Awakened Heart provides the tools we need so we can release the old habits, patterns, and rituals that hold us anchored in the old way of living. In detail, it shows us a path to follow that will enable us to begin to honor and value ourselves, and recognize our unique gifts and talents. If we follow this path, as Michael has so plainly illuminated it for us, at the end we may step confidently into the unknown.

Life is a process and so is this book. It is designed to uncover our essence so we can be who we are and freely express ourselves in ways we have only imagined thus far. A question to ask now is, "Am I ready to have the life I always say I want?" If so, then your journey to an awakened heart can begin right now.

Grounding Practice

The energy of the Archangelic Realm of Michael is a subtle and high-vibration spiritual energy. In order to facilitate a shift in consciousness from your ordinary way of perceiving, before you open the pages of this book to read further, Michael has provided a grounding practice. You may use the same practice prior to reading each message and doing each of the exercises contained in the book if it feels resonant to you. (You'll observe that much of what happens in this book relates to feeling.)

To begin, please find a seat in a comfortable chair. Sit upright with your feet grounded on the floor and your back supported. Then, simply close your eyes and feel. Breathe in through your nose and out through your mouth slowly three times. As you do, move into the depth and breadth of your heart, and connect with the essence of you.

If it is helpful, a few times you may silently, mentally repeat, "I release and let go." Then, fully release your thoughts from your mind. Know yourself simply as you are. Let go of looking for answers of how, why, and what you should do, or about trying to figure out or control the outcome of anything in your life.

For this practice to be effective there is nothing to do other than simply to allow yourself to be where you are, and to remain there as long as you need to, in stillness and silence, until you feel you have grounded into your being.

Rest and be you.

When you are ready, you may open your eyes and begin the journey of reading this book (or a particular chapter), which will take you even deeper into the depth and breadth of your heart to reveal gradually and more fully the essence of you. Moving through each exercise that you find here will bring you to a place of understanding, knowing, and loving yourself.

Part One
Who Are You?

You are already beginning to move in congruence with others in your life. You have made the decision to join your energy with theirs, thus taking the first step to move from a state of separation into a state of connection. You are already in the process of shifting from Me-consciousness to We-consciousness. Congruence is when aspects of your life overlap with aspects of the lives of others, like the fingers of two hands intertwined.

Through your personal process of honoring and valuing yourself at deeper levels, different energies within you are being joined. By going deeper in this way, you will shift your resonance and raise your vibration, and then move effortlessly forward towards the fulfillment of your soul's divine plan. At the moment you are reading these words, you are entering a process to learn who you are, and new ways to honor and value yourself.

On your journey through life, you have come to an intersection. It appears as if you have come to the end of the road. You are at the end of an old life and looking ahead to jump into a new life, but you are not sure what that new road looks like or where it will take you. The new road is your soul's divine plan. It is not a job or a relationship, or any one thing you are supposed to do. There are many, many facets to your soul plan and they come from knowing who you are. At the intersection, before you move forward on the new road, it is time to stop and look behind you at old attachments and patterns. Moving forward means leaving fragments of your old life behind. You'll know what they are.

You want to make a contribution to the world and live a life of meaning, to serve through your presence using your talents and gifts. But at this intersection you might be thinking, "Why undertake this task? Why do it? Truthfully, I am not sure what I have to give to world service." If you wonder, you only wonder because you have forgotten that you are the world as much as any other. Who you are being is how you are expressing your contribution according to your plan. By loving and honoring who you are and what you are doing, you resonate with your soul's divine plan and with the members of your soul family—those who share your vibration and are in harmony with your plan.

In the ten messages and complementary processes of Part One of this book, it is your work to release your attachment to the outer world so that you may move ever more deeply within and answer the question: who are you?

Message

There is a flame that burns deep inside you. It burns brightly and radiates outward from your heart with an effervescent energy. You now can choose to connect with this flame.

"I know who I am," you say. "I am ready to connect with my deepest passion." You may also have found yourself saying, "I no longer resonate with what goes on outside myself," even as you wonder how to disengage from it. You do not yet know how.

You have chosen the life you are leading...so here you are. The way to disengage from the aspects of the life you're leading that no longer serve you is to be present in each and every moment with what is. As you do, you will connect with your passion deep within that tells you why you are here, and your flame will illuminate your life.

As you begin to connect within, you might feel you need to know "how" it is all going to work out. "How in the world am I going to do this," you may wonder?

It is a process. Knowing yourself is a process first of connecting to yourself, leaving behind any judgment that stands in your way, seeing yourself through the eyes of compassion, connecting to your inner flame, and then radiating its spark into the world.

It is time to love you. It is time to move forward. The depth of your heart is awaiting you. Come join it.

1
Where Are You?

This process is a simple tool that you may use any time you find yourself immersed in a situation that is bringing up old feelings and memories, or old habits and patterns kick in that no longer resonate for you. When your ego defenses get triggered, you may use this technique to release yourself from the rituals of your old conditioning from childhood. Whenever part of you wants to escape, or a voice in your head carried over from the past distracts you, it is a way to take a momentary pause so you may ground yourself.

You know where you are when you are not triggered. But you might not know when your conditioning has a grip on you. This practice will give you clarity. Every soul that has clarity will be triggered at some point in the future, so practice this tool several times a day. It is designed to help you locate yourself in multiple dimensions of your being.

Begin to notice: "There is something I would like to change."

Since everything in life, including your thoughts and feelings, is a choice, with acceptance and compassion ask: "Where am I?"

Then, name five aspects of where you are.

Take out a piece of paper and a writing instrument, and make notes.

Example: you notice, I am always in the same place of financial scarcity? This is getting terribly uncomfortable I'd like to change that." So you halt in your tracks, take a deep breath, and name five aspects. Begin with "I am..."

1. Ready now to leave the old behind.
2. Repeating old patterns that keep me struggling to survive life.
3. Fighting deprivation. (Meaning, in emotional resistance to the lack of something that exists in your situation.)
4. Unsure why I am stuck.
5. Planning to reach out to the people who value me for help.

Next, ask, "What do I need? Could I take care of this need myself?"

How willing you are to state your needs depends upon the extent of your self-love. So you also ask, as a reminder, "How much do I love me?"

The underlying theme is for you to determine, "Am I important to me?" Given the fact that you are important, and that you want to change something in your life—one specific habit or aspect of your life—what do you need?

As you write down your needs on the piece of paper, observe your feelings. Answer this question: "How do I feel when I write down (or state) my needs?"

This process will help you find the places where you have been more committed to perpetuating old habits, patterns, and rituals than you were to facing your feelings, if you have shame and judgment about the feelings. You created your rituals long ago to avoid feeling, so ask two more questions:

"Is there a feeling I am avoiding?"

"Is there a habit I use to avoid it?"

Finally, now that you have discovered who you are being and what you are feeling and avoiding feeling in the moment, you are ready to clear the energy of your old life.

Ask:

"Do I want to change that?"

"Can I change that?"

"Am I willing to change that?"

This process is the first step of shifting old habits, patterns, and rituals, the first step in releasing the energy of an old way of life with which you no longer resonate. You are at the intersection of the new, the unknown, and it is important to know where you are in every moment as you are leading yourself forward.

Message

This series of processes leads you to making an agreement with yourself. In your current state of consciousness, you realize that the old no longer works. It is futile to try to fit a square peg in a round hole, and you are no longer willing to lend energy to that which is futile. Whenever you try doing things the old way, it doesn't work. You know you need to move into something new—a new career, a new relationship...a new life—but you do not yet know what that will be like.

The wounded girl or boy who lives inside you has guided your life to this point. It is now time to move into full self-individuation from Mom and Dad, to release shame and judgment. You will be moving now through a series of doorways. As an adult now, you may invite the child to walk hand in hand with you as you make this journey. You guide the child. Approach these processes with the intention to heal the wounds of the inner child to the extent that is resonant with your soul plan. Not everything is intended to be fully healed in this lifetime. You will heal sufficiently to fulfill your soul purpose. As long as you keep awakening to yourself you are doing as you intended to do.

Every doorway leads you deeper into a relationship with yourself. As you open the doorway, you are peeling away layers of a mask that protect you from experiencing feelings that you have stifled. You were taught that feelings have meanings. Feeling sad might have meant "being bad." Open the doorways and reclaim those feelings.

2
Open Another Doorway

You are now ready to take a series of gradual steps towards intimacy. You are beginning to trust—first yourself, and then others—as you break free from the cocoon of a life where you have held yourself in lack, limitation, separation, and isolation. Even as you say, "I want a much larger life than I have now," your next step is inward rather than outward. It is now time to open a doorway inside and receive love.

The intention for everyone who moves onto the pathway towards the unknown is to receive love—each of you says this is what you want. Look now to grow towards it, to embrace love from where you are. To achieve a community of harmony, acceptance, and compassion in the world, it is important to move within and begin to love you. With acceptance and compassion, you can be where you are in every moment and feel exactly what you are feeling, knowing that just being you is more than sufficient; it is essential.

When you hit a sticking point, such as a moment where you experience feelings you don't want to feel, or aspects of self that you don't want to accept or acknowledge, you habitually use something to avoid feeling.

What is your modus operandi for avoiding places in yourself that don't quite resonate for you anymore? What "old trick" do you use to avoid your feelings, to avoid being where you are? Do you put up a mask when you feel that who you are and what you are feeling in a given moment is not lovable? Do you use this mask in an attempt to be what someone else wants so you will be loved?

We speak to you about beginning to open your heart to receive love. You ask us, "How can I receive love? Am I good enough or worthy enough to receive love? Am I perfect enough to receive love?" This process is about moving to new depths of intimacy within, so that you can begin to receive love from yourself. It is most important to move through this process with tenderness because you could feel exposed and vulnerable.

Stand in front of a full-length mirror. We suggest that you do this process naked and learn to accept yourself where you are in the moment as you do. Of course, if you are not comfortable doing this exercise entirely nude, you may do it partially clothed.

Approach this exercise with an attitude of gentle curiosity. Every time you do it you open another doorway leading you gradually from your head to your heart. Take out a paper and pen so you may record your responses and discoveries.

Begin with your eyes closed. Breathe deeply into the depth and breadth of your body three times—in through your nose and out through your mouth.

After the third breath, inhale deeply a fourth time and retain the air for five seconds. Then release your breath on the sound, Ahhh." Allow the sound to reverberate through your entire body and through the room in which you are standing. Fully release and let go and allow the sound to move where it will move. Repeat twice more.

When the reverberations of sound have ceased, open your eyes and look directly into the mirror. As you look directly into the reflection of your eyes, breathe three times, inhaling through your nose and exhaling through your mouth with the sound, Ahhh."

Do not take your eyes off of yourself as you breathe. Feel the emotions that surface, and allow them to be present. Simply observe and take notice of what you do here.

Do you avert your gaze to avoid looking at yourself? Is there shame?

Do your thoughts become active? Are you judging and condemning yourself?

Do you suddenly think of an "urgent task" to do and walk away?

The idea here is to focus upon your eyes, and maintain an intimate connection with yourself. With your eyes still open and looking at you, after the third breath, if you are ready, write down what you are feeling in the moment. Move your focus into your heart, and then spontaneously write down the five most important feelings that surfaced.

After you have recorded your insights, return to the mirror and stand in front of it. If you are still wearing clothes, now is the moment to disrobe.

Close your eyes and breathe three times in a row, as you previously did. After the third breath is entirely released from your body, open your eyes and look directly into your eyes in the mirror again. Hold your own gaze for five to ten seconds.

Then, allow your eyes to travel and scan your body. Notice, where your eyes go first. Look at yourself. What do you see? What do you feel? What do you judge and shame? What do you enjoy?

Keep on breathing deeply. Remain in front of the mirror and scanning your body for several minutes. What might occur could be quite shocking to you. You might feel embarrassed. Or, rather than criticism, you might find you enjoy yourself immeasurably. Most importantly, you will begin to find out how you feel about your physical body.

When you are ready, sit down and answer the following questions:

"What am I feeling?"

"Am I shaming and judging? If so, what?"

"Can I accept with compassion where I am in this moment?"

"Can I accept what I am feeling in this moment?"

"Can I have compassion for myself?"

Now, move away from the mirror. Seat yourself somewhere comfortable and breathe once, deeply, and inwards through your nose. Hold the air for five seconds, and then release your breath through your mouth on the sound, "Ahhh."

After this, close your eyes and move into the depth of your heart space. Imagine your wounded inner child. When he or she comes to you look into the little child's eyes and remain focused on them. Look at them as he or she looks at you.

Feelings will surface here. Just be with them and allow yourself to feel what you are feeling in this moment. Then ask your inner child, "What do you need in this moment?"

After the child answers, ask yourself, "Can I give this child what he (or she) needs in this moment?" And, "Do I love this child enough to give the child what is needed in this moment?" Open your eyes and write down what was asked for, and your response.

Message

Time is of the utmost importance. There is no longer time or energy to waste on that which no longer supports your highest good or the highest good of the family of We-consciousness, the soul family of harmony and equality. It is time to take care of your needs and move forward. These teachings are quick and to the point for a reason: there is no longer any time to waste for those who realize that the old way no longer works.

You can no longer sit around and complain about the old. Now, it is time to stand in your truth. The earthly plane is shifting and changing rapidly. Aspects of what is happening in the physical world—earthquakes, storms, and the like—are clearing vortices of energy on the planet. More of this can be expected. It is being utilized to raise the vibration of the earthly plane. What you see happening in you, as a specific individual in the microcosm, is a mirror of what is happening in the macrocosm. You must break down the energy of your past conditioning in your mind to clear layers of energy around your heart.

Congregations of likeminded individuals are gathering throughout the world. Their hearts have been awakened and their mission, by coming together, is to raise the level of resonance and vibration of the planet by lifting their own. Wherever a specific group at a certain resonance congregates to pursue a personal process the resonance shifts. In whatever specific physical place they may be, a vortex of clearing opens.

3

Being Alone

You are now resonating at a level where you are moving within and beginning to gather your thoughts, feelings, and intentions for yourself. Now, it's time to fill your "toolbox" and learn how to use those tools. Some of you have already been given many tools. Some are apprentices learning how to handle them. Some are actively searching for tools.

The next tool in your toolbox is your sense of self. You are looking to step out onto the great pathway of the unknown and, as you look at it outside of yourself, you see nothing and this frightens you. Seeing nothing frightens you. It is evident that you cannot control anything outside of you. Seeing nothing on the pathway ahead means your life is simply about you now. You have been used to looking outside of yourself to have your needs met. Now you are looking within. As you are moving into the depth of your heart, you gather everything you know about you and all your energies to this one space.

You have shed layers of wounding. Now, it is as if you have moved into a closet within your heart where you are looking at rubbish. You have identified the old aspects of your life that need to be thrown out. You will keep shedding layers and tossing out the rubbish until all you have left is your truth and your energy.

"Who am I?" you may be asking. "Since I know I can no longer look outside of myself for validation and gratification or for anything, who am I now?"

Looking for a toolbox is to search for what you need to take with you on your journey (other than yourself). You ask, "What can I bring with me?" In your toolbox are the tools you learn in your life about being who you are, and honoring and valuing your wonderful self. When you hit obstacles, these are the tools you will utilize.

You are beginning to release the patterns of isolation, separation, and duality within you. And when you look into the mirror now, you are beginning to enjoy who you see reflected there, as opposed to judging and shaming yourself. You can look into the mirror today and say, "I like this person; there must be something to this process."

Old judgment and shame falls away as you integrate parts of yourself that you once avoided by honoring, valuing, and loving yourself from the depth of your heart. As you do this, energy emanates from your heart and raises the level of resonance and vibration within you. What comes next from you is a thought, "I would love to meet someone and begin to share this feeling with another soul." Realize that the person you would like to meet is someone who feels the same as you do. And once the two of you get together, you both will wonder what it would be like to meet another person...and another.

By raising your vibration and level of resonance you attract those who are resonating at the same level. By moving in harmony, peace, and love with the essence of yourself—in congruence with your truth—you connect with a community outside of you.

You are now moving out into the world on a new pathway with a somewhat intact self and looking to give from the depth of your heart, enjoying how wonderful and glorious you are. World service occurs when you begin to look for ways to express yourself and ask, "What can I give?" Understand that this is why you are looking to attract and be with others who are at the same level of resonance as you.

You are wondering, "If I love myself this much, what would it be like to love and give to another?" There is more to your life than narcissism. There is more to life than just getting, accumulating, and consuming things, and making it all about Me. You are ready to give. You have realized that you can give to yourself because you have moved through a process to gain tools that guide you to support yourself. You also now realize that it is time to serve the world. However, you might feel a bit confused yet about the relationship between giving to yourself and giving to the world. This is why you have a bag of tools.

You are learning to give and receive in balance. As you consider what is and honor and value yourself, you become deeply aware of your self. You gain a sense of self. Thus, you are gravitating towards a deeper sense of knowing yourself, and understanding what this means in every moment. Becoming clear to you are the talents and gifts you used to create your life. So, you wonder, "If I give of my talents and gifts, which enable me to convey who I am to others, what will I receive in return? What do I need?"

It is now time to open your heart and unlock the chains that surround it to reveal the depths of who you are. In a resonant community you may share your visions, yourself, your talents and gifts, and state your needs, set your boundaries, and express yourself to the fullest. It is time to "be" you and to live in a balance of giving and receiving with likeminded individuals from your own soul family of We-consciousness.

In the following process, begin to examine your relationships. Look at the people in your life and answer a series of questions to determine if those you are in relationship with are serving your highest good, and if you are serving theirs?

"Am I in these relationships to get something?"

"Am I giving something?"

"Am I in these relationships simply to remain in a comfort zone?"

"Am I frightened to be alone?"

"Am I looking to learn how to be alone, yet frightened to be alone?"

"Why am I in this relationship?"

"What is the relationship?"

"Why am I having this relationship?"

"Why is the relationship important to me?"

"Is it important to me?"

"What about the relationship I am having with myself allows me to remain in old relationships that no longer support my movement towards the greater good of myself so I can support the greater good of the whole?"

"Is there something far greater than the two of us that moves me towards something that has a meaning, value, and purpose greater than the comfort of our relationship?"

Look at the relationship you are having with yourself and ask:

"Is this relationship supporting my highest good?"

"Are the relationships I am having supporting my highest good?"

"If I am supporting my highest good in the relationship I am having with myself, am I supporting the highest good of those with whom I am having relationships?"

"Is their true intimacy in the relationship I am having with myself?"

"Is their true intimacy in the relationships I am having with others?"

Gaze at yourself in a mirror. Ask:

"Do I fully honor and value me?

"What feelings do I need to process to allow me to fully love myself and stand in my energy alone?"

"What does being alone mean to me?"

Take out a piece of paper and a pen and write down the definition of "alone" or "aloneness" that comes to your mind. Write the definition spontaneously from your heart. This is important because in order to connect to your soul's divine plan and why you are on the path of creating a new world, you must stand alone and individuated, honoring and valuing who you are. Liberate your mind, move into your heart, and spontaneously write down what comes to you. For some, the definition will surprise and astonish you.

Then ask:

"Am I alone?"

"Do I enjoy being alone?"

Jeff Fasano

"Can I be alone?"

"Can I truly stand in aloneness and know that I exist within it?"

"Can I give to me?"

"Am I giving to me?"

"Am I giving what I need to myself—or am I looking outside of myself to get what I think is not within me yet?"

"Is there something I could give myself that would allow me to stand alone, loving, honoring, and giving to myself?"

Message

You have the power to transcend your shame and judgment of yourself. What path do you choose to follow? Do you choose to travel into your heart or will you go directly into your mind and listen to the chatter you find there, voices that are remnants of what Mom and Dad said or did that you believed meant you were unworthy, unlovable, bad, and wrong? Thoughts like these are conditioned; meaning, what they say does not have to be the foundation of your reality. What is real is in the depth of your heart. Do you choose to move into your heart and look at yourself through the eyes from your heart?

You are ready to connect with your soul's divine plan. Therefore, we ask you to acknowledge your worthiness, your accomplishments, and the strides you have taken to arrive at this place in time. Look at where extraneous mental energy holds you in a place and renders your talents and gifts useless. Find what you shame and judge about you. Find where you can release the extraneous energy that surrounds you, so you can begin to step out onto the pathway into the unknown. You are allowed to have a new life. You no longer need to prove to anyone that you are worthy of it, you simply are. Move into your heart with acceptance and compassion and know that you are worthy to be exactly where you are. You are allowed to have the life that you have determined you want.

4

Whose Voices Are These?

Continue now by repeating the exercise where you look into the mirror (see page 10). As you recall, this exercise has two parts to it. The first part moves you through a series of breathing processes. The second part is done entirely nude and reveals deeper aspects of who you are. As you look at your reflection, judgmental thoughts and shameful feelings surface. Yet there is no one outside of you judging or shaming you. This experience lies within. You are encountering voices that reveal how you have been conditioned.

When you move into your mind, you hear voices: memories and conditioning from Mom and Dad where, on occasions when they were without acceptance and compassion, they shamed and judged you. When you first open your eyes and look into the mirror, begin to distinguish the old memories, patterns, habits, and rituals that you go through. Most of you, if not all of you, hear voices saying you are not good enough, not worthy enough, not perfect enough...and remind you of what you haven't done yet. "Can't you get any better? Haven't you gotten there yet?" the voices say.

When these thoughts arise in your mind, and negative feelings flood your body, you can take responsibility for your reality by looking directly into your own eyes and asking, "Can I accept where I am and where I shame and judge myself?" By doing this, you have the ability to move out of the mind.

Use the following meditation to release the conditioning, the old memories, and what you have learned from Mom and Dad. Use it to identify the voices and begin to separate what is myth from what is real. What is real is in the depth of your heart. And what is real in the present time is accepting with compassion the voices, judgment, and shame that have arisen within you, which represent what you have learned.

After you complete your breathing and your body scans, as previously described in lesson 2, move into meditation. Close your eyes and move your awareness within your physical body. You don't necessarily have to move into your heart space, you can simply move within. Ask, "Whose voices are these? What have I learned?"

As you identify these voices, write down whose you feel they are and where they are coming from. This will enable you to distinguish your mental conditioning from what is in your heart. It is important to identify each voice, if you can, because what you are identifying is actually a memory. See it. Hear it.

If you cannot specifically identify a particular voice or memory, simply acknowledge that you are hearing something. "This is in my head." Write down what you hear.

Then move into your heart. Ask, "Does this or doesn't it resonate? Does what I am hearing resonate for me now, where I am, as I stand in the depth of my truth?" Write down either "yes" or "no."

You can be sure that what lies in the depth of your heart is your truth. If the answer is "maybe," this exercise will help you determine your truth. That is its purpose. Ask yourself, "What is my truth? Can I accept with compassion where I am in this moment?" and write down your answers in your journal or on a piece of paper.

We also ask you to answer the questions about relationships that we asked you in the last lesson, the most important one being: "What relationship am I having with myself?"

It is vital that you continue using this exercise whenever you shame or judge yourself because it will be the jumping off point to moving towards the life you say you want.

Message

At this time you are now moving beyond the gateway. And, with some trepidation, you inch away from the gate and put a veil around yourself because you are not quite ready to introduce you with "who you are" to the brand-new world. You do this because you are not quite sure who you are yet and not sure what you represent. You believe your life is still about representing something. You are looking for something tangible to bring with you, something you will be able to show and tell those on the new pathway about who you are. It's as if to say, "Here is my résumé, this is who I am."

Your résumé is what you have done, what you have given, and what has transpired in your life beforehand, so you can prove who you are. And it is the veil you wrap around you at this time because you are still looking for something to bring with you so you can prove your very existence and value to those you encounter in your "new" life.

We ask you to look at what you are proving. Move within your heart and ask, "What do I still have to prove to those outside of me so they will know who I am and where I am going on the path?" It is as if you have been asked to bring along your passport in order to prove your identity. Know now that this is no longer needed and why.

5

Ten Aspects of You

Knowing who you are is the reason for the messages and lessons in this part of the book. We now ask you: who are you? And we give you a new writing exercise, which begins by asking yourself, "Who am I?" In your journal or on a notepad, you will then spontaneously write down ten aspects of yourself.

Do not ask, "What have I done?" Or, "What have I done for you?" These aspects are not your résumé, but who you know yourself to be. Instead, ask: "Am I giving? Do I listen? Am I present? Do I honor and value myself? Who am I that I can take my 'tools' with me and walk out on that pathway naked in the brand-new world just simply being who I am and without having to prove myself to anyone so they will love me?"

The reason why you still feel you must prove who you are to those outside of you is so they will love you for something you have done or given as opposed to simply being who you are. You might say, "Well, I am a wonderful entrepreneur and I give away thousands, if not millions, of dollars every year, so do you love me?"

This exercise is very simple. Have your paper and pen handy. And be near a mirror. We want you to do this for three days in a row, preferably in the evening before going to bed. At the top of a page in your journal write down the question: "Who am I?"

Jeff Fasano

To begin, move within in meditation. Close your eyes, ground yourself, and breathe in through the nose and out through the mouth, making the sound "Ahhh" on each out-breath three times.

After the exhalation of the third breath, take one glance in the mirror. Looking directly into your own eyes ask, "Who am I?

Immediately, write down ten aspects of yourself that you love, which will tell others who you are. If you can't reach ten, so be it. Write down as many as you can up to ten—no more than ten, however.

This exercise is about letting go of having to prove to others who you are. Like the preceding lessons, it is about going deeper into your heart space and discovering what you love about yourself. Who are you? Who do you know yourself to be? What do you love about you? The list includes who you are and what you love about you.

Give this list to yourself as a gift.

How much do you love yourself now?

Message

Now is the time to commune with one another in harmony, acceptance, love, and compassion. It is time to express yourself fully as you are and where you are. It is time to let go of herd consciousness. Let go of the myths perpetuated outside of you about who you are supposed to be. Unite with a passion that lies in the depths of your heart—and speak that truth. Express it!

Move within and ask, "What resonates for me? What in the depth of my heart do I need to connect with? Where is my passion? What is that passion? What is the passion deep within that I now need to connect with so I can affect change?"

As you are moving deeper into the depth and breadth of your heart, you can more confidently move forward and towards what you say you want. You are moving from the cause and affect aspect of living your life into a life governed by resonant causation.

Ask, "Can I now connect with my passion in order to individuate and speak the word that is mine and mine alone? Can I now connect with the passion deep within me in order to move forward and towards what I say I want, know, and can do to change the world in which I live?" You see now that it is you and you alone who can affect change through changing within yourself. "Speaking your word" is being the truth of who you are.

Ask, "Can I now hold myself responsible for the impeccability of my word as I utter it to those outside of me who may look to me for the support and guidance they need?"

6

What Am I Feeling?

Now it is time to begin to feel your feelings on a regular basis. These feelings are very real, and, if you are allowing yourself to feel them, you are coming to know that not only does the truth of your life lie within the depth of your heart it also lies in your feelings.

You are undergoing a maturation process from wounded child to self-mastered adult. As you give yourself the freedom to feel your feelings with acceptance and compassion, you will begin to move into a place of greater self-empowerment. No matter what feelings come up, you will embrace them and begin to enjoy feeling them. And, as you do this, you will naturally begin to integrate them. Your resistance to specific types of feelings that you once thought were "bad" will diminish. It is important to know that what you are feeling is not who you are; your feelings are simply feelings. As you move past resisting them, you will also move beyond the drama and glamour they represent.

In allowing yourself to experience the depth and breadth of your feelings, you may occasionally feel afraid as you move towards what you want. In the past, this fear would cause you to move into resistance. But as you allow yourself space to feel a feeling, you simply can walk through the feeling and continue moving towards that which you would like to manifest in your life. Stepping into a place of empowerment, you can be who you are fully because you are simply allowing yourself to feel your feelings.

You move into true adulthood when you heal the perception of the little boy or little girl inside you who actually thinks he or she is what he or she is feeling. For example, if you are feeling "not good enough," the little child thinks he or she is not good enough. If you feel angry, the little child thinks he or she is an "angry person" and yet is not permitted to express it. When you feel your feelings, you release the memories attached to certain feelings of Mom or Dad telling you that you aren't allowed to feel.

All people have different feelings that they were conditioned to believe it is wrong to feel. Some believe it is not okay to feel anger. Some believe it is not okay to feel sad. Some believe it is not okay to feel joy or enthusiasm. Some believe it is not okay to feel vulnerable or to love. Each time you give yourself the freedom to feel the feelings you have avoided—and as you allow yourself to feel these feelings again and again—you are empowered. With this empowerment you will begin to move swiftly and boldly into the unknown.

Your resistance to your feelings has held you back in your life; it has kept you stuck in an experience of lack and limitation. Until now, you made resisting your feelings more important to you than that which you say you want. The truth you are discovering is that you can move swiftly toward what you say you want and feel your feelings at the same time. In doing so, you are releasing duality within your perception. Duality is the perception, "Either I do this or I do that. Either I feel a feeling or I resist it."

If you move toward what you say you want and you do not allow yourself to feel your feelings, ultimately you will reach a moment where you will sabotage your movement towards the new simply because you are committed to resisting the feelings. You will remain on the hamster wheel of lack and limitation until you realize in the depth and breadth of yourself that you can simply bring your feelings with you wherever you go.

It is most important to understand this in the very moment a feeling surfaces; for your feelings are an aspect of your truth in every moment. How you feel will help you in discovering what and who you resonate with, so you can move forward.

In order to reveal your truth, ask, "Right now what am I feeling?"

Then answer: "I am feeling sad, anxious, happy, fulfilled, angry…and so on." Practice naming your feelings as they arise one after the other. "And now I am feeling…And now I am feeling…And now I am feeling…."

Employ your tool of breathing. When a feeling comes up that makes you feel afraid, resistant, or uncomfortable in any way, simply tell yourself that it is okay to feel it, breathe through it, and move the energy of the feeling with the sound, "Ahhh."

This is your most basic tool, tool number one: breathing with sound. This will allow the energy in your body to flow so that you can move towards what you say you want by being in the moment of truth and being who you are in that moment.

"Right now I am feeling sad," you might say to yourself. "I know who I am. I know what I say I want. And I am moving towards having, doing, or being it, even though I am feeling sad." The more you practice feeling, the more comfortable you will feel with feelings you formerly judged wrong and avoided. You will integrate those feelings into your experience and thus you will allow yourself more space for being who you are.

After reading the last lesson, for three days you wrote down ten aspects of being you that you love. Part of that exercise is to learn to let go of explaining why you love what you love about yourself. Your list of ten aspects you love always should be short and to the point: "This is what I love about me. This is who I am."

We ask you to continue this exercise, and now, after completing your list, to go one step further by asking yourself, "How does this make me feel?" and " What do I feel right now?" Then, write down your answers.

What we ask you to do is to look into your eyes in the mirror and read the ten aspects you love about yourself out loud. Feelings will surface. Notice that different voices come along with these feelings. After you recite the ten aspects, sit down. Close your eyes and move within to a contemplative state. Breathe three times, utilizing the sound of "Ahhh" on your exhalation, and then ask your new question, "What am I feeling right now?" Spontaneously write down all of your feelings— and also allow yourself to be with them.

Take a moment to connect with the wounded little child inside you who is feeling feelings that you once would have resisted feeling, and ask the child, "What do you need?" When the child begins to tell you, allow the child to speak as long as he or she wants because many needs are likely to appear. Be as open as you are able to be to this experience. And write down everything the little child asks.

Then, look at what you have written, and ask:

"How do I feel about this?"

"Can I now move forward and toward what I say I want even with these feelings alive in me?"

"Can I give to myself whatever I need in this moment?"

Continue doing this exercise, preferably before you go to sleep at night. This is your chance to see that you can respond to your needs in each and every moment.

Be with your feelings no matter what they are. Your feelings will reveal your truth in each moment. They will also reveal what you have resisted and what has held you in lack and limitation—meaning, at a distance from having what you say you want.

Message

You are beginning to move ever so gingerly from the darkness into the light, and yet, like others, you may be experiencing a deep darkness in your world. While you are now beginning to maneuver your way through the darkness in your life by utilizing your new inner tools, others may not yet. Some are edging their way through the darkness with trepidation, wondering what it would be like on the other side. Most are searching for the light outside of them. During this period on Planet Earth, it is common to look out and wonder, "What is going on out there? Why is it happening? How is it affecting me?"

It is natural for everyone who stands at the inter-section of the old and the new to move through a shadow period in life. For if you who are, it is time to grab a flashlight and shed some light on the shadow, your resisted parts. You now can integrate the shadow, for it resides in the light. And you will soon see that the light resides in the shadow.

As you now maneuver through the aspects of your "shadow self," you do so by committing to practice the personal processes we have given you. Be aware to see if you become content to languish within the world you once knew by looking at the old rhetoric and paradigms which fortify the old way of life. You see the old as either/ or, good/bad, and right/wrong. This is duality. So see if this is resonant with the truth of who you are being now.

7

The Shadow, the Myth, and That Which Resonates

At this juncture, we would ask you to write down five aspects of the shadow in the world that no longer resonate for you. What are the old paradigms outside of you—patterns, habits, rituals, structures, and beliefs—that you resist experiencing? We ask you to take a good long look and then write down these five things that you do not accept or embrace.

When you are immersed in the shadow, in resistance to your feelings about what is happening in the world, you are in the depths of low-vibration resonance. So, also look at the world to see what is outside of you that you love and want to experience. Does it resonate with what is maneuvering within you towards the light? There is energy emanating from within the depth of your heart, and you are not necessarily sure what it is. Is it a soul murmur? Is your heart murmuring to you of a promise that would fulfill you?

Also write down five aspects of the world that do resonate for you.

You are moving from a life driven by cause and effect to a life of resonant causation, which requires you to feel so you may intuit what the best path for you to take is. This is why we asked you in the preceding two exercises to look at ten aspects of being you that you love and to identify how you feel about them so you would know.

All we are asking you to do now is simply to look at the world outside of you and ask, "What resonates for me?" And, "What doesn't?" Then make two lists containing five items each. One list is what resonates and one list is what doesn't. Then read them.

It is time to discover your truth and look at what you believe the truth to be. Is truth emanating from the depth of your heart? Or do you believe what others "out there" tell you is the truth of your life, is real, is right, is wrong, is black, or is white?

What others say is the truth may not be your truth. It may be a myth for you. That is why, by using this tool, you will be empowered to recognize the truth for yourself.

As long as you are in resistance to your truth, then you will experience a reflection of your shadow in the world. But that which you can accept within yourself will bring light to the shadow. It will raise the vibration of your energy until through resonant causation you begin to see the world around you reflect the shift. It can happen in an instant.

Knowing what resonates for you, how much do you love yourself?

Message

You are now beginning to emerge from the darkness and from the shadow of the old self with its old habits, patterns, beliefs, and rituals. The last exercise we gave you was to list five aspects of the world that do not resonate for you and five that do. We now ask you to look at the list you pay most attention to. Do you pay most attention to what doesn't resonate or to what does? Do you look at what is lacking and not present? Do you look at your glass as half empty? Or do you choose to look at where the glass is full, at what does resonate for you that is already present in your life?

Does anything resonate for you? And did anything once resonate for you that no longer does? Where do you focus your energy? Are you trying to figure out why certain things no longer resonate for you so you can find a way that they will? Or are you able to simply notice what doesn't resonate, release those things, and move on to what does?

Learning to let go, to locate yourself and embrace where you are, will free you.

8

For What Are You Grateful?

In practicing the lessons in Part One, thus far, you have gained a great deal of knowledge about yourself. You are discovering the truth of who you are and what you love about yourself. You are rediscovering shadow aspects of yourself through allowing yourself to feel feelings that you formerly resisted. And you are learning that you can move forward to having what you say you want and feel all of your feelings simultaneously. Perhaps you have been experiencing the surfacing of old habits, patterns, beliefs, and rituals that would serve to sabotage your progress and keep you from moving forward in your life.

We would ask you to continue using the tools we have given you if and when they are necessary. As you step forward on your pathway to the new, these will help you to find your direction when you stumble or feel lost. You can never be lost with these tools. Simply breathe and ask, "Where am I? What do I feel? What resonates for me now?"

Fighting lack and limitation will keep you stuck because lack and limitation are myths, illusions, not real. The absence of something is not real. Only what is present is real. So, as opposed to trying to escape or move away from that which does not resonate, mastery comes from focusing on the list of that which does resonate in your life. This will raise your level of vibration so you can move towards having, doing, and being more of what you love. Therefore, it is always important to ask these two questions:

"Where am I placing my energy and attention?"

"Am I focused on the absence of something or on the abundance of everything?"

When you stop looking outside of yourself for answers, and focus within you begin to embody more of your talents and gifts. You begin to see that you are the key to bringing that with which you are resonant into being in the world. Your energy, meaning who you are being, is central to resonant causation. It is the key to creating the life you love.

A most powerful way to move from your mind and into the energy of your heart space is to selectively place your attention on what you love. Ask: "What is in my life? For what am I grateful?"

Make two lists. The first will be your gratitude list. This can be an ongoing list that you make every day or if you decide to pause and shift your energy to a higher vibration. The second list will be a list of talents and gifts that you possess and can embody, which you can utilize to move you forward and towards the five aspects of the world that you resonate with and love.

Look at where you focus your attention and energy. Do you focus on what isn't there? Do you focus on the "negative" aspects that you perceive in yourself and in others? These are one and the same. Do you focus on the myths others tell you about what is and isn't true. Do you focus on what you read in the newspapers or hear and see on television and believe that it is real? Have you reflected upon what you are being told and shown and asked if it does or does not resonate for you?

Do you look at what you love about you and focus on what you love and enjoy in your life? Does how you are living and what you are doing resonate for you?

These two new lists will lead you to utilize your talents and gifts in service to yourself and by extension to the world. You are part of the world after all. These lists will help you identify the talents and gifts you have within you that can help you change the world so that it is more resonant with the energy of what you love.

You are ready now to use your knowledge of what doesn't resonate for you as a learning tool. This is your stepping off point to take the list of what does resonate for you, that which you have and enjoy and for which you feel grateful, so you may bring these things into the world by utilizing your talents and gifts.

You have a list of ten aspects you love about yourself.

You have a list of five aspects of the shadow (in the world) that are myth for you.

You know that what you have resonates more for you than that which you lack.

You also know how to respond to your own needs— you know how to give.

So, where are you focusing your energy? What are you grateful for? What talents and gifts do you have that would enable you to bring the ten aspects you love most about yourself into manifestation in the world?

Darkness is when you feel as if you have lost your way. Your resonance lowers. Gratitude helps you find your way. It raises your resonance.

It is time now to be the unique being you are, to do what you say you would like to do, and to bring your talents and gifts to the world. There is no time to spare, and yet there is no rush. There is no time other than the present. It is important to move forward and towards all the aspects of your greatness and to choose to bring to that world with every breath you take, even if that forward movement means feeling that which you have resisted in acceptance and compassion. Be grateful for being there for you.

Message

As you now emerge from the darkness the level of your vibration is rising within. It is as if a current of white light has descended upon you, and you are being swept up in its flow. You may choose to go along, because this current of light empowers you to release the old. Since you have released much of your old reality, you may feel you are in a place of nothingness. Yet you have never been closer to that which lies in the depth of your heart, which is the ever-expanding light.

Light workers are being invited to move towards this light that leads them on the pathway into the unknown. Some have moved beyond the gate of the new. Some have stopped and turned to look behind them at the old. Others still engage in the old and will remain there. But the old must be released by any who would move forward towards the light. Along this horizon of light lies the unknown. Its frequency is infinite and therefore it raises the level of vibration within the heart to infinite dimensions; it is an infinite realm of probability that has always existed and yet is more accessible now.

Your choice is simply this: will you, as a light worker, now choose to utilize your talents and gifts to move forward and answer the call from the depth of your heart to live in the unknown with the light? Can you allow that light to shine upon your pathway as you move forward into a world of harmony, equality, and community?

9

Twenty-one Days of Gratitude

You now are moving from a realm of possibility to a realm of probability, from a realm of questioning to a realm where things really happen. Between the realms, you are faced with a decision: do you make the choice to remain in the old, repeating old habits, patterns, and rituals, or do you move into the new, swept along with the current of light?

Last we came to you, we asked you to name what you are grateful for. Have you recognized that your talents and gifts are what you can use to create the life you say you want, and to contribute as an individual and collectively to building a new world? Are you now ready to release the narcissism of Me-consciousness, where everything you do is about "Me" in isolation? Now that you know who you are can you place yourself in the midst of the "We"? Can you see that you are not alone, that others share your path?

You are almost ready to begin the process of rediscovering your talents and gifts, and of understanding how to use them for the purpose of world service. Before then, however, you must undergo a period of entraining your nervous system to "What Is" as opposed to "What isn't." This entrainment will continue for the next twenty-one days.

Once again, we would have you write down what you are grateful for, and expand the same list every day to include new insights and discoveries. At the end of each and every day, write down one or more aspects of your life that day for which you are grateful.

This practice will help you to be conscious of what attracts you and of where—and with whom—you are resonant. You are now at a place to move with the light, to entrain yourself to higher vibration energies that are moving within the environment around you as your new world is beginning to emerge. So you are being asked to find what resonates most strongly for you in your relationships and activities, and to focus upon it.

When you do this, be sure to move into the depth of your heart and notice what you feel and allow yourself to feel it. It is time to feel everything. Be grateful for the opportunity to feel and to be with the truth of you. Following high-vibration feelings like gratitude will open the doorway to the new world that is being created by you and by those who share your resonance. It is your choice to entrain your energy.

Message

As you see the light and move towards it, you can see that the darkness you are emerging from is the shadow of an illusion of safety and security, a false sense of certainty you had in your life that your old habits, patterns, beliefs, and rituals would protect you. You are emerging from wondering who you are to knowing who you are, and you understand that being who you are is not only safe and welcomed by the world, it also is needed.

If you have been applying the tools we have provided you, you are no longer in the place you were when you began reading these first ten messages and exploring these first ten lessons. You now have such a firm connection in the depth and breadth of your heart space that you are ready to remember and reveal your talents and gifts.

That is why you are here.

10
Take Inventory

Before you move on to the consideration of why you are here in Part Two, it is important for you to take stock of your life. Write down your answers to these questions.

"Where am I?"

"What is in my life?"

"What do I have within me that I love about myself that I can give to others?"

"What can I open to receive from others?"

"A new world is being created; do I want to play a part in creating it?"

"What can I give now that will contribute to creating the new world?"

"Where might I create peace, harmony, and community?"

"With whom do I resonate?"

"What talents and gifts do I have?"

"What do I love doing that I do well and can give?"

"What have I created in my life so far?"

"What commitments have I made to bring me to where I am right now?"

"Have I been looking outside of myself for validation and gratification?"

"Have I been looking outside of me to get something to feel safe and secure?"

"What am I grateful for?"

After taking inventory based on the previous questions, then ask: "As I am now looking at what is in my life, what are the feelings that come up?" Move within in meditation, release your mind, move into your heart, and begin to just feel. As you take the journey into your heart, you will begin to realize your passion. Ask:

"What is my passion?"

"What brings me the greatest joy when I give to others?"

"Does it give me joy when I give to others?"

"Does asking another, 'How are you today?' bring me joy?"

"Does giving support and guidance to another bring me joy?"

It is essential you know the answers for your next step is into We-consciousness. Ask:

"Is it still about me?"

"Am I looking for others to give to me so I can take from them and move into solitary confinement within myself where I can consume it all?"

"Am I giving to others?"

"Do I receive joy from giving to others?"

"In doing so, am I receiving what I am giving?"

People often fear receiving love, so you may have a fear of intimacy. Thus, it is important to evaluate if when you give, you receive. When you give from the depth of your heart, are you sharing just a part of you with another or all of you? Are you opening your heart to receive another? Can you walk arm in arm, hand in hand, shoulder to shoulder into the unknown with another? Are you capable of giving and receiving in balance? That is the goal among people creating together, since balance and flow are one and the same.

Remember, before you can give, you must know what you have to give. Therefore, the next series of messages and lessons in Part Two, "Why Are You Here?" will take you on a journey of recognizing, remembering, acknowledging, honoring, valuing, and focusing on your unique talents and gifts. Throughout the journey, we advise you to continue to be with you and be who you are, and simply to do your best to be unto those outside of you as you would like them to be unto you—this is Me and We in balance.

Part Two
Why Are You Here?

After discovering who you are, the next step is to determine your talents and gifts. What do you love? Have you connected to the passion within your heart and found what brings you joy? This is not a question of how you bring joy to others, but of how you prefer that joy comes to you. Once you have connected with your passion, you can confidently say, "This is what fuels me and this is why I am here." And it will be true and manifest.

If you know who you are and your purpose in life, your clarity will begin to draw a soul family around you that resonates with a similar mission and purpose as yours, and your life will begin to look more like that which you say you want.

Message

As you now move forward to create a new world of harmony, community, and equality, your life has become about giving in order for change to take place in the world. By standing in the truth of your essence, you have raised the level of your soul note. Through living your passion, you are calling your soul family to you. These are resonant souls with whom you will walk arm and arm, shoulder to shoulder into the unknown new world.

We ask you to move into your heart and imagine a ray of golden-white light there. You are at the gateway to the unknown. Join your heart with the hearts of others in harmony and community to receive support and guidance for one—and for one and all. Breathe deeply inwards as you imagine this ray of golden-white light moving into the center of your heart, and watch the gate swing open as you breathe out .

11

The Joy of Giving

Having begun to move into the depth and breadth of your heart, you are ready to release yourself from the total influence of your mind. What is happening is this: you are leaving behind a lifetime of needing to figure everything out before you do it, of searching outside of yourself for validation of who you are and for gratification, and of worrying that you are not enough. You are leaving behind the superfluous baggage of the stories that have kept you immersed in an unrelenting drama of overcoming lack and limitation. You are ready to let your mask drop and allow others to know you as you are.

As you move into the space of living your life from within your heart space, it is as if you are entering the first grade and gathering with other little children. None requires you to plan what you have to do, how you will say what you say, or who you will be. They all accept and embrace you as you are because they are also being who they truly are.

You are on a journey now to connect with the light that is inside you. And even though this journey is taking you into unknown territory, you are safe. You have in hand all of the tools you need to open your heart and mind wide to receive your answers, to receive life. The moment has come. You are now ready to discover why you are here.

The unknown is a space of nothingness. Your life every day from now on will be about constantly beginning over. It is essential that you follow your feelings. Faced with the possibilities that exist, where you are in each moment is always the beginning. And where you are is always where you are in this moment. So begin again. Every moment compounds preceding moments. You understand this. And from knowing this, you also know who you are, which brings the next question: Why are you here?

"Well, I thought I was here for this or for that, Michael, but now I am not quite sure if it is true," you could say. Most people have similar doubts. You may be wondering, "What should I do now? What do I have of value within me that I can give in service to the world?" These questions are natural extensions of your earlier explorations.

The question to return to is: Where am I? Follow this up by feeling your feelings. If you remember to continually open to the depth and breadth of your heart, you will access feelings that help you to discover your talents and gifts, and new ways to apply them.

With compassion and self-acceptance, ask:

"Can I give?"

"Have I given in the past?"

"Do I take joy in giving?"

"Where does giving excite me?"

"What can I give?"

"What do I have to give now, moving forward as I am into the unknown with my heart wide open?"

You will discover your answers as you read the ten lessons here in Part Two.

Begin now.

Move within into an inner space of silence and meditation.

What are the five most important aspects of your talents and gifts? Make a list in your journal. When you're done, look at your list and read over these aspects. Then, repeat the questions above: "Can I give? Have I given in the past?…"

Be with those five aspects. Get in touch with your feelings. Move at your own pace. There is no need to rush through this process. Whenever you feel ready, ask:

"What do I do well?"

"What do I like doing?"

"What in my life brings me the greatest joy?"

"What do I love doing that brings me joy?"

"What is my passion?"

"What have I always dreamt of doing that I might like to do?"

Write down your responses. Your list could be one, two, three, four, or fifteen things.

Next, zero in on the single most important item on your list by asking: "What do I love doing that brings me the greatest amount of joy and raises the level of resonance and vibration within me when I am doing it? What is this?"

You will know it because it is something that radiates from the depth and breadth of your heart. Write this down and then simply be with it. Sit with it for a moment.

Have you discovered your passion? Have you discovered what you love doing the most that brings you the greatest amount of joy? Once you find it, ask:

"How does it make me feel?"

"Is this something I could do right now?"

Write down the answer yes or no. Then, feel your feelings. That's all it takes.

If you notice that you are having thoughts like, "You can't," inquire of yourself what holds you in the space you are in of not-having, not-doing, and not-being.

"What holds me in this place?"

"What are the old beliefs?"

"What have I been taught?"

No matter what you believe that is holding you in limitation, please understand that you no longer need to defer to it. You can live your truth. What passion came up for you? This is what you now are available to give from the depth of your heart.

Message

The unknown is simply the unknown. But it is time to determine if you can now fully allow yourself to be who you are while facing the unknown. You are in an entrainment period, entraining yourself to be who you are because, in fact, you are all you have. As you move onto the straight and narrow pathway into the unknown, creating a new world of harmony, community, and equality—and your new life that coincides with this—you are all you have. So are you harmonious and equal and in community within yourself?

You now have a bag of tools and you can trust that it will continue to fill up as you make your commitments. These tools will guide and support your movement forward and toward having more. But, as always, the most important factor is to feel your feelings.

You are always and forever doing only one of two things. Either you are having what you say you want or you are avoiding the feelings that are surfacing inside you. In order to have what you say you want you must be willing to feel these feelings. For as you move forward towards what you say you want, your feelings will get stronger until they reach a crescendo. All the shadow feelings that you ever wanted to avoid will come to the fore now, into the light; they are there for you to embrace and integrate.

12

What Do I Want?

You are now moving forward on the straight and narrow pathway that lies beyond the gate. After looking at what you are grateful for, and considering everything you have in your life, you are armed with all the tools you need to step forward confidently into the unknown. But it is time to make a definitive commitment so that you no longer have to meander around trying to figure out what you are here to do. We are purposefully guiding you to clarify, define, remember, and discover your commitments.

You have taken the first step to release ambivalence about making a commitment to what you say you want and what you say you are here to do. Nonetheless, you still have some degree of trepidation. As you move into the "new life," recognize that the "old life" revolved around the myth of control. In your old way of doing things, your thoughts were focused on trying to control everything that lay ahead of you. You no longer need to do this now for one important reason. The difference is that you know who you are now. Everything "out there" in your life continues to be unknown, as before, but because you know who you are you are ready to form a new life in a world of harmony, community, and equality.

Jeff Fasano

Maybe you thought you had already committed? Actually, you are just at the first step of making a real commitment to having that which you say you want. Could you make a commitment to move forward on the straight and narrow? Could you commit to letting go of your ambivalence to moving beyond the gate because of fear of the unknown? Any fear you experience is just a fear of feeling the feelings that surface in the face of the prospect of having what you say you want and doing what you say you are here to do.

This brings you now to the next exercise in this series of lessons aimed at discovering why you are here. We ask you to write down what you say you want. Ask:

"What do I want?"

"What do I want out in the world?"

"Am I having what I say I want right now?"

"Am I truly having, living, and being what I say I want?"

"Am I being true to who I am?"

"Is my heart open to receive all that I want?" (If it were, you would, in point of fact, already be having what you say you want.)

The next thing to do is to explore your commitments and intentions. Ground yourself with three breaths as we taught you and then bring yourself to where you are at present. Write down the answers to the following questions:

"What do I say I want?"

"What do I actually want?"

"Considering this, what would I say I truly want?"

"What have I said I that I have wanted all along?"

"Are these things the same?"

"Am I truly having what I want yet?"

When you are done writing, close your eyes, move within, and picture and sense yourself having, living, and being what you say you want. When the picture is clear, continue by asking:

"What am I feeling?"

"Am I truly feeling the feelings that are coming up in me?"

"Am I feeling not good enough, not worthy enough, not perfect enough?"

"Am I looking outside of myself for something to validate and gratify me?"

"Do I know who I am?"

"Am I being who I am and opening my heart, even as I take the next step towards having what I say I want?"

Remember, this process is not supposed to be a gallop, a jaunt, or a race. It must begin with offering yourself acceptance and compassion for where you are and for what you are feeling in the moment. It is not a race to get somewhere so you can have something that will validate and gratify you. This is your life, a life to live, a life to give, a life to be. Your process is your life.

We will fervently continue to ask you to feel your feelings as you live your life. Always consider: "Where am I? What am I feeling? What do I say I want?"

Having done this exercise, please ask one final question:

"How much do I love myself now?"

Message

Energetically, you are moving into the world most fervently and you may be feeling a bit overwhelmed by following through so swiftly and intensely on your passion. If you have shifted from your heart back into your mind, a sign of this is wondering, "How can I do all of this? How will this manifest in my life? Why isn't it manifesting right now? What am I doing? What do I have to do? Why am I here? Why am I doing this?" When you sense a shift to increased mental activity, pause to reflect and move back into the depth of your heart to look at yourself. Calmly check and see if you are honoring and valuing who you are. You can do what you love if you embrace your needs.

13

Where Are Your Boundaries?

Let's touch upon the matter of personal boundaries. Have you set your boundaries—emotional, energetic, and physical limits that you place between you and other people—based upon honoring and valuing yourself? Is it possible that these boundaries are lines of demarcation? Or are they malleable and responsive to conditions? Are your boundaries rigid and unresponsive to conditions, causing you to isolate yourself and frequently find yourself in conflict with others? Or are your boundaries almost non-existent, so that you lose your sense of yourself, ignore your needs, and say yes when you want to say no? You are learning to speak your truth now so that you can look at another and simply say, "These are my boundaries." The way to set appropriate boundaries in the moment is by honoring and valuing yourself and your truth.

In Part One, we gave you an exercise of writing down ten aspects of yourself that you love. We now ask you to do this again because today you are in a different place than you were physically, mentally, and emotionally the time you originally did the exercise. Now that you have come to a new place, again ask:

"Where am I?"

"What do I honor, value, and love about myself?"

"What are ten aspects of me that I love?"

After writing down these aspects, continue by asking:

"Do I honor and value these aspects of me?"

"Do I fully honor and value me?"

"Could I look out into the world and set boundaries based upon what I honor, value, and love about myself?"

"Am I telling those outside of myself who I am or am I assuming they know it?"

"Am I speaking my truth?"

"Am I speaking my truth out in the world based upon who I am and what I honor and value about myself?"

"What are my boundaries?"

Boundaries are lines drawn in sand rather than cement, because they can and will change. The idea is to base them upon honoring and valuing yourself and where you are in your life. So it is important to reflect on how the conditions in your life have changed. What are some boundaries you could set where, for example, you might now simply say to someone, "This behavior is no longer acceptable to me based upon where I am."

The issue of boundaries ties in with current relationships. It is important to look at where your relationships are shifting based upon the ten aspects of you that you love. As you have changed, have your relationships changed as well? Having raised the level of your resonance and vibration, do you now need to set new boundaries?

Do you even fully understand what boundaries are? It is important to understand the nature of boundaries because you will use them going forward to contain your energy.

Look at what no longer resonates for you and look at what does. The ten aspects of what you love about yourself are places where you resonate. You have created a new you. Who is this being? Do the ten aspects you love reflect this new being?

This is your opportunity to review where you are. What has shifted and changed in your life? What is continuing to shift and change in your life? Look at how you have been affected by this shift and how you have manifested the change. You are beginning to stand in your power, to move forward and manifest what you want. In order to do this to a greater degree, out in the world, you must know both who you are and how much you love yourself.

There is a difference in knowing who you are through your ego and knowing who you are through self-love. Knowing yourself through the ego (the old way) was about separating yourself from others. If you say, "I know who I am—and I am better than you!" This is a form of superiority and it creates separation. It is not equality. It creates a need for validation and gratification from outside of yourself.

Loving yourself as you are (the new way), on the other hand, allows you to stand unmasked—with your energy contained. Knowing and loving yourself allows you to walk on the path into the unknown just as you are without creating isolation.

Jeff Fasano

Having boundaries leads to balanced giving and receiving in relationships. It means you can say, "I love me and, therefore, I can love you. In turn, our relationship has balance and equality; it empowers me to speak my truth to you when I have a need to set a limit or take care of myself, and it empowers you to say the same to me."

Boundaries are part of the foundation of community, harmony, and equality. They lead to clear agreements and to having your needs met.

Define your boundaries. What are yours? Make a list. Then, ask:

"Am I setting boundaries or am I building walls to isolate and separate myself?"

"As I set my boundaries, am I listening to others who set theirs?"

"Am I honoring others' boundaries and my own?"

"Can I listen to others when they set boundaries?"

Look at what you have accomplished and created for yourself. Look at your life as being full. Is there joy in it? Are you walking on your path into the unknown feeling joyful about what you are creating—not so much joyful about what you are creating in the world (which relates to seeking validation and gratification), but joyful about who you are creating within yourself? If you have committed to know and love yourself on a deeper level, you have committed to individuate and take responsibility for yourself. Setting boundaries is another step in taking responsibility—of responding to your needs.

The purpose of this lesson is to look at your life and see what you love about yourself. In the mirror, look directly into your own eyes and begin to receive who you are now. Love yourself so you can begin to take the next step to love others.

Message

The world outside of you is cacophonous. Things are changing rapidly and it is easy to get caught up in them. It is more important than ever to move within on a regular basis, so you may entrain yourself to be who you are. Do you still look around and wonder how you can fit in "out there"? Asking "When and how will everything manifest for me?" just keeps you caught in the cycle of seeking validation and gratification. Instead, go inwards and entrain your energy by connecting with that which you love. Learn to trust yourself.

As you entrain yourself to be you, and lovingly respond to your feelings and needs with acceptance and compassion, your talents and gifts will be revealed.

14

Five Aspects of Self-love

As you continue this journey, the core of your heart is beginning to reveal itself and to unravel as well. The depth of your feelings is now being revealed; feelings that you have not allowed yourself to feel, yet now are beginning to entertain. These feelings coincide with your old habits, patterns, rituals, and attachments. With every old attachment there is an old feeling. And the reason why you continue these old attachments, patterns, habits, and rituals is entirely due to your way of relating to these feelings. As you entertain old feelings, you will find yourself repeating old habits, patterns, rituals, and attachments.

We ask you now to look at your relationships and your attachments to them. Do you wonder why you are attached to certain relationships that no longer resonate with you and why you stay in them? Feelings will come up if you ask, "Although it no longer resonates with my requirements for a relationship (because my boundaries are not being honored or my needs are not being met), why do I continue this relationship?" As feelings arise, consider another question: "If I moved away from this relationship how would I feel?"

These two considerations are an example of what is happening to you now as you entertain feelings that you never wanted to feel and fully resisted until now. Entertaining these feelings now is shifting your resonance and, as a result, the structure of your different relationships is undergoing a transformation. How you relate to yourself is changing. How you relate to your work is changing. Everything is changing.

The most prominent evidence of how you are shifting is seen in your relationships. Even if you can plainly see that a relationship or a habit, pattern, or ritual does not serve your highest good, the old pattern may persist. Therefore, it is important to ask:

"What am I doing?"

"Why am I doing it?"

"If I stopped doing it how would it make me feel?"

Going into the depth of your heart to feel your core feelings will enable you to release old habits, patterns, rituals, and attachments so you can move forward towards living the life that you say you want to live and discovering your soul purpose.

You may already be using your talents and gifts. Yet you have questions. If so, we ask you to look at what you are doing. Do you love it? As you continue to embody your essence, the meaning, value, and purpose of your talents and gifts will be revealed. Your talents and gifts are simply an extension of who you are. So they are becoming clearer. It is time to embody them. As you embody your gifts and talents, and continue to love and honor yourself ever more deeply, you will no longer need to use your talents and gifts to gratify yourself, get validation, or prove yourself to those outside of you. You only need to be who you are. You are enough. When you love yourself fully, it will be plain to see that your talents and gifts have a purpose, a value to give to the world.

In entraining yourself to be you, your talents and gifts will begin to take on a new shape. They will develop. In an organic fashion, you will begin to realize why you are here. This all begins with you and what lies in the depth of your heart. You can begin by moving though remnants of the old, especially in your relationships.

Perhaps you are feeling frustrated. "Michael," you might say, "I am stuck in the old. I am not moving forward towards having the life I want as quickly as I would like." You feel as if your life has gone out of control. If you thought your life was under control, frustration is surfacing now that you have realized you do not really control anything.

As you walk on the pathway into the unknown and creating the new, you are not in control of anything because the unknown is unknown. Nothing is actually there.

You will create a new world of harmony, community, and equality simply by being who you are and utilizing your talents and gifts. Why you are here is revealed by taking the next step into the unknown and moving through feelings that you have avoided. If you feel stuck, you can get back on the pathway to having what you want by taking step after step. This is why we asked you to look at what you love about yourself because it is easy to wander off the path. The path is the commitment you make to who you are.

Jeff Fasano

In the human condition, everyone would love for things to happen instantaneously. It is human to want instant gratification. However, stepping into your soul's divine plan is a process. Many of you thought you had a plan, but this plan is not your soul's plan. Your soul plan is out there for you to discover. It comes to you as you create and embody your talents and gifts. It comes to you simply by being who you are.

We ask you to look at your relationships. Are there any attachments in them? Where do you focus your attention? What habits, patterns, and rituals persist in your relationships? What feelings come up when you realize what you are doing?

Look at your old relationships to see if they do or do not resonate for you. You are going through a clearing process, clearing out the old ways that no longer serve you. You are in the midst of a period where you are faced with the residue of the old ways and old feelings. And it is time to encounter these feelings, to feel them so you can release your old habits, patterns, rituals, and your attachments to different relationships.

As you now begin connecting with your new soul family, we ask you to look at those with who you are already in relationship. As your heart is opening, many of the people who are coming into your life are not quite how you pictured they would be. You are encountering more diverse people than you have ever known. It is important at this time to keep your heart open as you create your new soul family. Look at the new world on the horizon even as you continue moving through the shadow and facing your old feelings.

Move back within now and re-connect with yourself. Throughout the next week, make a point of writing down five aspects of you that you love every day. And make a list of your gifts and talents. Creating both of these lists side by side will help you relate to your talents and gifts in a brand-new way. Consider how you can use them to give to the world. You are now ready to segue into fully embodying your talents and gifts. But first you must introduce yourself to their depth and see how you are using them.

As you begin to fully embody the truth of who you are, you will become more aware of how your different talents and gifts express who you are. Look to see if you are using your talents and gifts to be noticed, to prove who you are, or to gratify yourself. Look for ways to embrace and embody your talents and gifts and use them to give to the world.

You have power within you. When you know who you are, this power will allow you to manifest anything you say you want simply by being you.

Message

You can speed your progress now by streamlining your efforts. You are in the midst of a process of moving from a state of narcissistic "Me-consciousness," where everything is about you, to a state of "We-consciousness," where nothing is ever about you except for how you embody your talents and gifts and where you choose to utilize them. Knowing who you are means that you can just be you in every moment. If you know that what you are offering best expresses who you are and what is important to you, then you already know the meaning, value, and purpose of what it is you have to give to the world.

15

Are You Ready?

As you move deeper into the core of your heart, feelings are being revealed to you that you have long avoided feeling. It is essential to become conscious of them. This period of your life is a time of great shifts and change, and it is all taking place within you. It's as if you have come to the edge of a precipice where you must decide to take a leap into a new life. You must make the decision to shift and change within or to remain where you are.

Having moved through the process of coming to know who you are, you are now at a place to put why you are here into action. However, before you can do so, you must "grab the bull by the horns" and commit even more fully to discovering your talents and gifts. Fortunately, as every talent and gift is revealed to you, a coinciding feeling will also be revealed—and that feeling is joy. You are uncovering talents and gifts that resonate with who you are in the depths of your heart. This is why earlier we asked you what you enjoy doing. And it is why we ask you, again, to consider the questions:

"What do I enjoy doing?"

"When I give, what am I doing that I enjoy?"

"What are the talents and gifts that coincide with this joy?"

"If I am doing this and I enjoy it, how am I doing it?"

"Am I just doing it or is a specific gift or talent allowing me to do this and express who I am?"

Understand that nothing is separate. You can enjoy whatever you are doing. You can embody what you love in everything you do. So, as you do what you do, notice if you are enjoying it. Investigate where the passion is in this activity. Two questions are helpful:

"If I wasn't doing this, what would I be doing?"

"Would I rather be doing something else?"

It is time to focus on the meaning, value, and purpose of everything you do. So ask:

"Why am I doing this?"

"What is the meaning, value, or purpose of me doing this?"

"Is it to get something or is it to give something?"

"Is it to prove who I am or am I being who I am?"

"Am I giving from the depths of my heart to serve the greater good?"

"Am I giving to serve another wonderful and glorious soul?"

We now put you on notice that from this point onward the exercises we give you will be aimed at streamlining your commitment. If you choose to continue, the commitment is not an arbitrary act on your part, it is a lifelong experience. Commitment is a perpetual experience. What we mean is that each and every time you move within and ask yourself, "Where am I? What am I grateful for?" and continue practicing the other tools you have learned, you are perpetuating the experience of you. You are moving deeper within, to the very core of your heart, and along the way you will feel feelings that you always have avoided. But eventually your commitment will lead you to experience joy.

You have come to a point where you need to make a decision. Is it more important for you to resist certain feelings that come up or is it more important to have what you say you want? This is the place where you have arrived. Your choice will be an indication of whether or not you are in the process of leaving the old life behind and moving forward towards a new life of harmony, community, and equality. No one can make this decision for you. And if your choice is to remain in the old way of life, so be it.

The soul group you will be forming in the new life you create will be based solely upon the resonance and vibration of each of the individuals who enter into it. You have already shifted your level of resonance by going through the process of discovering who you are. Your soul group will be formed with those who are at the same level as you; like you, they will be raising the level of resonance and vibration within them. Some people currently in your life will make this choice, others will not.

You may peek through the doorway to the new life and wonder, "What is going on, on the other side? I have a choice to make. Is it really important for me to create a world of harmony, community, and equality? Is it really necessary to cross this threshold?"

If, looking through the doorway, you feel reluctant to step through it, know that those on the other side of it welcome you. These individuals feel you, know you, and love you, and they will be there to support and guide you; this is the way of a soul family. You are supported and loved, felt, seen, and known.

Are you ready? The next step is the step of forming your new soul family. First, however, you must choose to relinquish the old, to move into the new, and to feel your feelings as they come up. Continue asking:

"Where am I?"

"Who am I?"

"Why am I here?"

"What am I grateful for?"

"What are my talents and gifts?"

Look into a full-length mirror and ask, "What do I love about me?"

Write everything down.

Then ask, "Do I choose the old or do I choose the new?"

You are poised at the edge of the precipice to make this choice. From this point forward, those who continue on the path will have made a clear decision.

As this process continues, the road ahead might get a little bumpy. So it is imperative to have conviction. Conviction comes from making a firm commitment. So is your decision to continue on the pathway or is it to engage, indulge, and sink? Is it the new or the old?

What is being revealed now is your power, the power of you.

You can have it if you choose it.

Message

You've made a choice to move further into the unknown and to decipher the resonance of your new soul family. You have made the choice to create the new world of harmony, community, and equality and to change the world that already exists. If you say, "I want to change the world outside of me," then you must change the world inside you first, for the outer world is only a reflection of your inner resonance.

It is important to stress accountability and impeccability. Become impeccable with your word to yourself. This is about you and not others. It is time to fully profess that you are leaving the Narcissistic Me behind you—the old patterns, habits, and rituals—for you are now well along on your pathway into the unknown and have moved through the doorway. The door is only just closing behind you because there are still fragments of the old that need to be put to rest. Then, the door will close. It is up to you to know your singular purpose in this lifetime, to state that purpose, and to be accountable.

16
What Gives You Joy?

This lesson is about joy. Are you enjoying your life? Are you enjoying who you are being in your life? Do you enjoy being where you are in your life right now? Are you enjoying the path of moving forward towards what you say you want? Or do you still struggle to survive aspects of your life, and perhaps enjoy fighting lack and limitation because this fight is familiar to you? Is it possible you are confusing joy with safety and security?

The next exercise is simple. Ask and answer these questions:

"What is joy for me?"

"Is there joy in my life?"

"Can I look at five aspects of myself that I love and feel joy?"

"Do I judge and shame parts of myself?"

"Can I look at five aspects of my talents and gifts and feel joy?"

"Do I judge and shame my talents and gifts?"

You have done exploration to discover who you are. And in doing so, do you now take joy in knowing who you are or do you continue to indulge those feelings which you have long resisted and avoided by perpetuating old patterns, habits, rituals, and attachments to relationships where your needs are not being met?

Do your current relationships bring you joy or do they enable you to keep sinking into your feelings and perpetuating old habits, patterns, and rituals?

Is there a relationship in your life that is a perpetuation of an old pattern, habit, and ritual? If your answer to this is yes, where are you in this and where are you attached to the old?

Joy is a natural state of being. Does being you bring you joy yet?

The task now at hand is to consider: "What is joy for me?"

Write down everything that joy is and means for you. Describe your joyousness in detail from every situation you can remember.

As you do this exercise, it is most important that you fully immerse yourself within, for this exercise is a tough one for most people. You are likely to hear voices in your head that will come up to edit and censor your joy for you. Feelings that you have long avoided, ignored, and denied will surface.

What do you feel? What is your first reaction whenever you begin to feel joy? And what are the feelings that are coming up now?

Write down the word "joy" on a piece of paper, and then write down all the feelings that arise simply from having written down this word. What immediately comes up? Do you hear voices guiding you to deny the fulfillment of what you say you want?

Joy simply means feeling fulfilled within the depth and breadth of your heart. You experience it by filling yourself up with you—by knowing who you are, by being who you are, and by feeling all of your feelings. Joy is you fulfilled by knowing what your talents and gifts are and knowing that you are giving these to the world just by being you.

Although joy is stimulated by the people and situations around you, it is never received from the outside. Joy is fulfillment from within. Joy is not learned. It cannot be taught. It just is. You naturally are joy.

Having looked at your joy, how much do you love yourself now?

Message

We have said to you, the process begins with you releasing the layers of armor around your heart and moving into the essence and the truth of you. You have found that to a certain level—the level is different for each person and will remain so. Yet you are now ready to release your narcissism and focus upon building a new soul family based upon your resonance and vibration and sharing a similar purpose. You are forming a new family based upon true self-expression along with the impeccability of the word in the communication of that expression.

How do you choose to speak to your brethren? Can you now put yourself in your brethren's shoes and fully see the mirror there to take responsibility for you? We ask you always to begin here. Look at yourself in the mirror first, then take responsibility for your part of your relationships, express yourself, state your needs, and set your boundaries. Look at yourself first, as opposed to looking at what another is doing, might be doing, could be doing, should be doing, or would be doing, for focusing those concerns only leads to drama and glamour. Are your endeavors creating community, harmony, and equality through joy? Is there joy in drama and glamour? Is there joy in anything that reduces the level of resonance and vibration? Look at your past and see what you have seen. Look at what has transpired to see what has reduced your joy. Look at your past and what you have learned, at the gifts and lessons, as you are faced with a new beginning.

17

Painting Your New Picture

At this most important time, we ask you: what are you utilizing to paint your new picture of the world and the life that you say you want? What are your brushes?

We are here to speak to you about your tools, your talents, and your gifts. Which of these are you are using to paint your new picture as you move forward towards the new world of harmony, community, and equality that you are creating?

You are at the edge of the precipice about to take a leap into the unknown, and here at the edge you are beginning to form a new soul family by opening the depths of your heart to see what and who resonates for you. Where are you, right now, as far as your talents and gifts are concerned? Have they surfaced yet? Where talents and gifts are concerned, what is bringing you joy? Have you recognized and remembered them?

Once again, we ask you to write down your talents and gifts. Make a list of five specific talents and gifts that you are using to create a world of harmony, community, and equality around you. Ask then answer these questions:

"What am I doing for myself with my talents and gifts?"

"What talents and gifts are enabling me to give to myself in the same ways that I give to others?"

"When I am giving in the world am I receiving love in return?"

"Or am I using my talents and gifts to get whatever I am looking for—to keep me safe and secure, to win a struggle to survive, to overcome lack and limitation?"

"Am I getting only enough in return for my giving to survive life?"

"Is the way I am utilizing my talents and gifts simply perpetuating and maintaining my old habits, patterns, rituals and attachments?"

Having reflected and answered on paper, now answer these questions:

"What am I feeling when I recognize my talents and gifts?"

"What am I feeling when I give and receive?"

"What am I feeling if I do give to get?"

It is certain that you are doing some variation of giving to get. Most people are both giving and receiving, but they are not primarily receiving love in return.

This exercise will allow you to begin to perceive the truth of what you are doing, so that as you move forward towards your new life, it will include a balance of giving and receiving. First, however, it is important to recognize your talents and gifts and value.

Do you love who you are now? Do you love what you have discovered about yourself? Do you love who you have discovered? Do you love the wonderful and glorious soul, you, who is utilizing your talents and gifts? This is where you are now.

As you recognize more about your talents and gifts, do they bring you joy?

At every moment in every day look and consider:

"Where am I in this moment?"

"Am I giving in this moment?"

"Am I receiving in this moment?"

"What am I feeling in this moment?"

"Who am I being in this moment?"

Going forward, we ask you now to practice daily meditation. Most importantly, before you go to sleep each night do a recapitulation of your day. Every night, reflect upon the questions: where am I? What transpired today? You do not need to write down your answers, although you may do so if you so choose; more or less you will simply be reminiscing about your day to increase your awareness. We use the word "reminisce" purposefully, rather than the word "scrutinize" because it is important to reflect without judgment: where did I step into my greatness? Where was I angry? Where was I sad? Where was I? Where am I? Who am I?

At the end of each and every day now, briefly reminisce.

It is most important to continue doing the exercise on a regular basis in order to entrain your energy and teach you to focus on what you are creating. It is also important that you begin to solidify your talents and gifts. Your talents and gifts will grow as you continue to move deeper within the depth of your heart and rediscover who you are.

You have just begun to scratch the surface of a continuous process of self-discovery. Who you are manifests in each and every moment in each and every day. So move into meditation at the end of your day, and spend five or ten minutes reminiscing.

Can you accept what transpired during your day? What did you learn about yourself and others? What did you learn about your talents and gifts and where did you use them? The idea is to begin to notice how you are responding to whatever happens—are you continuing your old habits, patterns, and rituals or flowing with resonant causation.

It is time to fully encompass all that you are with acceptance and compassion for being where you are. This is what this meditation does. Ask, then answer:

"Can I accept where I am each and every day?"

"Can I see the growth from where I was to where I am now?"

"Can I move within and begin the process of deepening the love of self, the love of who I am, so I can now begin to open the door to create the new soul family?"

"Where am I?"

"Who am I?"

"What do I say I want?"

What gifts and talents are you utilizing to paint the new picture of your life and create your new world, the world you say you want? Are you doing it?

You may have the misconception that your talents and gifts are specific skills you can utilize to do something for others or that enable you to get something. But can you see now how you are using your talents and gifts in every moment, in every situation, and in every interaction with another wonderful and glorious soul?

It is time to see that your talents and gifts are not only skills you employ, but you simply being who you are. They are what you use to express your being. Your talents and gifts are simply a tool that you utilize to express the depth and breadth of you. Giving of who you are through your talents and gifts allows others to find out who they are so they can be that. Then they can find their talents and gifts and relay them to others just as you are doing.

Can you simply move into meditation, look at your day, see what transpired, and reminisce about it? Release shame and judgment, and stop scrutinizing your every move. You are where you are and exactly where you are supposed to be in your process. Ask:

"Can I accept this with compassion?"

"Can I joyfully accept where I am?"

"Can I now ask this question: can I change?"

"Can I commit to continually changing where I am?"

Changing where you are is the key to the creation of the new world.

Message

You are now moving into a final phase of your transition, a time at which you will be able to make a choice about where your life is headed. This is an individual choice; you are releasing having to look outside of yourself to see what everyone else "out there" is doing and wondering if you should follow suit. You are beginning to let go of being a follower; letting go of those who in some way, shape, or form you have deified; and letting go of those who you think have the answers you need or hope will lead you to the Promised Land. This aspect of your transition is about releasing being a follower so that you can move into the depth of your power, greatness, and self-knowing; so you may lead yourself. We have guided you to a place where you can become a way-shower for others who are looking for guidance and support as they enter the intersection to the new.

You are moving into congruence with multi-dimensional energies in order to find the frequency in the fifth-dimension that you resonate with so you may connect with the energy and messages, and pass them on to your brethren who are coming to you. Be sure to allow these messages to assist and guide you where your talents and gifts are concerned. You are on an accelerated path and there is neither time nor energy to waste on that which no longer supports your highest good. Your highest good is you living your purpose.

18

Walking the Path

As the doorway closes behind you, your life begins to be created through resonant causation. Having made the decision to walk within the energy of the new, you now have a chance to release every last remnant of the old. But as the new energy mixes with the old, it can feel like a chemical reaction is being set off. For some, this energetic mixture can become volatile. You are no longer able to control anything in your life and so it is important to surrender entirely to what is. You are now consistently living a moment-to-moment existence. Thus, continue asking yourself, "Where am I? And what is?"

You are likely to feel quite anxious and nervous for a while. The door behind you is sealed shut, but the door to the future is still unlocking. The future is just being created by you. You may feel some trepidation if you still lack full understanding of why you are here. Even as you are discovering why you are here, you may wonder, "How will I use my talents and gifts?" Know that your answer will begin to formulate as you concentrate on moving forward towards your new life on the path you are currently walking.

You are beginning to connect to your soul's divine plan in the depth and breadth of your heart; be assured that the pathway you are on currently leads to it. Some people are further along than others, but everyone reading this assuredly is on this pathway. You have already made the choice to emerge from the old life and step into the new.

Look at yourself in the mirror. Can you not see that there is no going back? This is why your feelings are becoming more intense. You are in resistance to moving forward towards the life you say you want because you have moved out of your deep-rooted comfort zones, where you were looking outside of yourself for validation and gratification. This behavior no longer resonates for you and therefore it is non-existent on the pathway into the new. Nothing outside of you can give you gratification any longer—and this may frighten you. "Where can I go to satisfy my addiction to getting something from outside of me?" If you look into the mirror, you may see nothing. Many people, as they look out onto the pathway into the new, see nothing. Nothing is actually there except you.

Use what you have within you as your well of fulfillment. What you created by doing the preceding exercises is in your well. The well inside you is filled with who you are. And the well is becoming deeper as you discover more of your talents and gifts. Can you utilize you as you move to create the new world of harmony, community, and equality?

You are resonating and vibrating at a new level, and possibly you are looking at old relationships that no longer resonate and vibrate with the new you. Are you still looking at what is unavailable in your life and hoping that those who are unavailable to what you say you want just "get it" and come along for the ride? Can you open up to the unknown and let the wonderful and glorious souls come to you who are your new soul family? Are you willing to release old relationships that do not fulfill your needs and create new relationships with those who are available? Through resonant causation you will be able to create relationships based in love as opposed to attachment to what you can get. You can also create new relationships with those from the old life you led who are moving on a similar pathway. Some from the old are no longer walking the same pathway as you. They are on the other side of the doorway and wondering if it will open again.

We ask you to continue the exercise of writing down five aspects of your talents and gifts that you love. Also continue your nightly meditation where you reminisce about the events of your day. By doing this you will begin the process to learn how to receive love.

Are you giving to yourself? We will add one more aspect to your process. Each and every day do something good for yourself. You are on a new pathway and it is no longer a dark passageway into the unknown. It is now well lit, even though it may be unknown. For some, the pathway is still empty. For others, it is already filling up with wonderful new creations and glorious souls who now call themselves your brethren. These are people who resonate and vibrate as you do, and are open to you if you will stay open.

Look now at what is most important for you to release in your life. What is hanging on that you would call "excess baggage"? Is there an unnecessary output of energy on your part in certain places? Where are you expending energy on what no longer serves your movement forward towards the life you say you want? Are you expending energy where it no longer needs to be? Releasing whatever is unimportant to the new you will hasten the creation of your world of community, harmony, and equality.

The doorway behind you is locked and sealed; there is no escaping into the old way any longer. You have made the choice to become the light worker that you have often said you wanted to be. Are you committed? Are you now moving forward from the depth of your heart filled with love? Unconditional love is love given with full acceptance and compassion. This does not mean that you have no boundaries or that your needs are not stated. Unconditional love is full acceptance and compassion for you, as well as others.

As you love yourself more, you will do the things necessary to take care of yourself mentally, emotionally, physically, and spiritually. This is love: loving you.

As you move through your human experience, you will hit "blind spots." This is why we ask you to reach out to others for support and guidance as you move forward in your process. Ask for support from like-minded individuals who are on the pathway to create the new world of community, harmony, and equality. Receiving support and guidance is of the utmost importance. The old pattern was, "I can do this alone." We are here to tell you that this is no longer a viable option. Always remember the need for community.

As you are nearing the creation of your new soul family, be aware and conscious of your old biological family patterns, where separation, isolation, and duality existed. The new soul family holds in place community, harmony, equality, acceptance, compassion, and loving from the depth of your heart. Join now with others to raise the level of resonance and vibration in the world. This is done first within you, then within the group, and then it will be done en masse out in the world. This is the pathway you are now traveling and have chosen. Is this now your truth?

It is now important to live your life with integrity and impeccability, for the new life is about love. You are finding love—not so much the love of another, but a truer sense of self that is based upon love. It is time to open to your brethren and join your energy. Open the doorway to your heart to allow those who resonate and vibrate to walk through it, so you can meet them. You are ready!

Message

Why have you undertaken the endeavor and the path to self-mastery? Are you doing it just so you may tell everyone you are involved in a process? Or have you undertaken this process to know who you are, to honor and value your talents and gifts, and to know your purpose? Are you accepting the role of light worker so you can give to the world in order to shift the level of resonance and vibration of the realm you have chosen to incarnate in as a human being, the third dimension? Are you moving through the process of self-mastery to give to those outside of you who are coming for your guidance and support? What do you now need to join the legion of the light workers?

19

Receiving Love

Begin to walk through your life with joy.

You have walked through the shadow and through the doorway into the unknown. The door has closed and is now locked behind you. For a period of time, your deepest fears of safety and security surfaced. "Will I be safe in the unknown?" "Will I be safe with myself and trust myself in the unknown?" As you now walk gingerly into the unknown, you're not sure what is going to happen and this will bring up the aspect of control. You are now out of control and living in your natural state of being for out of control is a natural state of being. Now that you are being guided to live with "what is" and in the moment, where are you?

Where you are might not be anywhere. You are where you are and quite possibly have no explanation for it. You have found yourself in situations with wonderful and glorious souls where you could explain where you were and who you were. But now you find this is no longer a viable option. It is more important to remain in the process of moving towards the place where you connect with your soul's divine plan. For after you reach this place, you will be presented with a new choice of whether or not to continue on the path to entirely be who you know you are.

There will no longer be a thought process involved if you stay on the path. You will simply be who you are. And, in being you, you will be the messenger for the messages that come to you. You will utilize your talents and gifts to express the messages and who you are. Where you are now is in a process of releasing whatever you still need to release to continue on the pathway towards this intersection.

We come to you now to bring you to a place to receive love from yourself. Continue writing down five things you love and adore about yourself because this will allow you to begin to receive. But now, after you make your list, move within and feel your feelings. Also write down these feelings. How does any aspect you listed make you feel?

While doing this exercise, you might find that you are still looking at "what isn't there yet." Or you might find that you are looking at "what is there" and experiencing a deep sense of fulfillment and joy. Fulfillment of being comes when you can say, "I know who I am; I know my talents and gifts." When you arrive at this place, proceed to look into the mirror to receive yourself and to give love to you.

Continue to give yourself something every day. Do something extraordinarily wonderful for yourself. Plan a point in every day when you will do this. Make a date. For example, decide, "I will give myself a wonderful gift at seven o'clock tonight." See if you keep your dates. Also notice what comes up for you when you are just about to give to yourself? What happens? Do you celebrate yourself or do you do everything in your power to avoid receiving from yourself? Can you give to yourself every day?

The only way you can receive love from another is by giving it to yourself first. Can you do this? Have you been doing it? It doesn't have to be the same time each day.

Your heart is beginning to open at a depth that you have never known before. Moving towards real intimacy with yourself, you are beginning to share who you are openly. The next step is to receive love from others; yet the first step is giving love to you.

Can you love yourself enough to know what that feels like, so you can then give to another? The only way you can give without attachment, to give without having to get something, is by giving to yourself first and receiving that love. You must know how that feels. So after you give to yourself, write down your feelings. How does it feel to give to you? Are you simply doing it because we are asking you to, and saying, "Since this is part of the process, it will get me somewhere—Michael said it would"? If this is the case, in essence what you are doing is giving to yourself with an attachment. "If I give of my talents and gifts, then I will be gratified and validated. Others will love me. They will see that I am good enough, even perfect, and then deify me if I do this right."

Give to yourself, and give consciously. Be conscious of how it makes you feel and notice if you are giving to yourself in order to get or to get rid of something. You may find that you are wondering, "If I do this exercise, what will it get me?" or "What will doing this exercise enable me to get rid of, which I can't accept with compassion?"

You are at a most important time, for in order to move forward you must know how to give love to you. This is where you are and it is important. You have discovered and remembered many talents and gifts and you are now at the place to begin to embody them and love those parts of you that you express using your talents and gifts. Now you are ready to open to the depth of your heart to receive love.

It is also time to move through your life with joy. If you are one of those who have chosen the path of the light worker, it is time to look at your meaning, value, and purpose because this is shifting and changing. There is a new purpose, which is to give in order to create a new world of harmony, community, and equality. What is the new purpose for your talents and gifts? After you write down the five aspects of your talents and gifts that you adore, also ask yourself, "What is their purpose?"

As you move forward, there is yet another decision to make. Your first decision was to stand at the gateway to the new. Once the gate opened, your second decision was to walk through it and onto the pathway into the unknown.

Soon you will have the opportunity to embody your soul's divine plan. This is your third choice. You will reach an intersection where you may connect fully with your soul family. As you have raised the level of resonance and vibration within you to get to this point, you connected with those who were close to the level of energy and frequency as you. Now you will have the choice to gather with those who resonate and vibrate at the same level, those who share the same mission. If you decide to embody your soul's plan, everyone in this soul family will have individuated, they will know who you are, and they will recognize their uniqueness as well as each other's uniqueness.

You are just beginning to move to the core aspect of your heart to begin to uncover the frequency that lies there. The way in which to do this is through this personal process you are now engaged in. This is a process of clearing, cleansing, and releasing what no longer serves your highest good and impedes your movement forward towards the realization of your soul's divine plan. There will come one choice to make: either to connect with the soul's divine plan and move on that pathway or not.

Message

You are, in fact, here to be a messenger, to shift the energies around you. You are here to change the world by raising the level of resonance and vibration within you, and by supporting others to do the same. You are at a most crucial point because your world is rapidly shifting. Do you resonate with the change or with what is old? Do you resonate with the change that you intend to make within you and your commitment to that?

The only way you can change what is outside of you is to commit to changing you. Commit to looking at all the aspects of yourself that you would like to change.

Who are you? Why are you here? Do you know who you are? Do you love you? Can you love you? Can you love yourself enough to commit to change while you are on the path? Can you commit to opening your heart wider than you ever have before to reveal who you are and give your talents and gifts to the world? Can you open your heart even wider to receive the love that comes when you give without attachment?

Receiving love is your purpose. Being who you are is all that is necessary for you to receive love. Give the energy of harmony, community, and equality and you will share love in a balanced exchange of giving and receiving wherever you go from now on.

20

The Final Phase
of Transition

You are now in the final phase of your transition, whatever that transition may be for you. You have joined different energies in your heart and begun leaving your old way of life behind. Therefore you have now come to this place, which is the place of endings.

On this pathway, you have found yourself. You love yourself more deeply now than you have ever known. The core of your heart is open at a depth deeper than you have ever understood was possible. You are beginning to understand yourself, you know who you are, and you embody this in everything that you do and say.

A new soul family is ready to be born. You are seeking to connect with them and them with you. You are ready to grow, to be who you are, to love yourself, to bring your talents and gifts out to the world, and enter into a new form of relationship. So, in this moment we give you the following meditation to do.

Close your eyes and move within. Breathe deeply and connect with the depth and breadth of your heart. Enter a place of silence, of community, harmony, and equality within. When you arrive there, open your eyes and respond to these questions.

"Where am I right now?"

"Do I enjoy where I am?"

"Am I living my life with joy?"

"Am I celebrating myself?"

"Am I celebrating who I am?"

"Am I celebrating what is here in this moment?"

"Can I look at the glass as half full?"

"Can I even look at the glass as being entirely full?"

Ponder these questions. Then, close your eyes and connect with your heart again. When you're there in your heart space, open your eyes, look around you, and ask:

"Where am I?"

"Who am I?"

"Why am I here?"

"What is the path I am on?"

"What is the new foundation that I have built for myself?"

"Where am I headed?"

"Am I looking toward the future?"

The future is where you will connect with your soul's divine plan. Once you connect with this, you will simply be who you are. You will no longer know it, you will be it.

Who are you today? We have taken you through a series of steps to find out, remember, and rekindle the spark of who you are, which means we now come to the end of this series. Have you remembered and rediscovered your talents and gifts? What are the five that are most important to you? How does knowing this value make you feel?

You are living at a most important time for your world. Look at everything that is going on outside of you and ask: "Does this support my movement towards changing the world and forming a family of like-minded souls who share the same mission as me?"

It is time for you to receive love. This love comes from you giving it to yourself and receiving it from yourself first. What are you giving to you? Are you consciously giving something extraordinary to yourself each and every day that shows your love?

Are you ready to implement the purpose for why you are here? You have made the journey from your mind into your heart. When you enter the core of your heart, time does not exist. What exists in this place is love. When you are in this place, you can simply observe what is happening outside of you. Anything outside of you will shift and change in its resonance in relationship to the depth of your heart. The resonance within the depth of your heart is quite different from the resonance or absence of resonance in the outer world. What lies within is your truth, and that is love: love of self and love of others.

To look outside of you and see what resonates for you and what doesn't, first move into your heart and see what resonates there. Then, ask and write down:

"What in the depth and breadth of my heart is ready to shine ever so brightly, which I just might have been covering up with a coat of armor?"

"What is now ready to shine out into the world?"

Any time you look outside of you to fight and defend yourself lowers the resonance and vibration in the depth of your heart. Engaging with the lower vibration of what or who you are fighting gives energy to that thing or person to engage with you. The transition you are making is not a fight or a battle; it is about shifting your frequency. Adhere to the resonance in the depth of your heart—this is the resonance of your truth—and love who you are. When you begin to do this, the resonance and vibration of the world around you will automatically shift in response. What is outside of you is simply an illusion, a myth. Your life and the world is always what you make it.

In finding your purpose, it is most important to move into the depth and breadth of your heart, as we have asked you to, then to look outside into the world and ask, "What resonates for me out there and what doesn't?"

You are a light worker. The reason why you have chosen to move to a higher level of vibration is to begin to counterbalance the perpetuation of fear. Are you resonating with peace, harmony, equality, love, acceptance, and compassion? Can you fully embody who you are? Can you look at what fear perpetuates outside you and ask, "Is this fear real for me?" Are you afflicted with illusions about the world outside of you? Can you see that what you are creating on your current path is a new world of harmony, community, and equality where fear no longer exists and only love, acceptance, and compassion do?

Can you perceive the sacredness of all life? Can you listen to your animal kingdom, your plant kingdom, your mother earth, and what your environment is telling you? The old habits, patterns, and rituals of the human are to think you know everything and must tell everyone, and that you must defend your rightness at all costs. What you now can begin to do is open your heart to listen and respond with what resonates there. When you listen to anything or anyone outside of you, listen to find what resonates for you so you can shift and change your own vibration. You are part of the sacredness of life.

When you are listening, are you hearing what is being transmitted? Are you receiving it? Can you hear it, receive it, and then respond to it? By responding, you and others will come together as We. Responding from what vibrates in the depth of your heart is love.

Consider what you need to do to take responsibility for yourself. Ask:

"What are my responsibilities?"

"What do I need to shift and change in my life so I can respond after I have listened, heard, and received information?"

As an individual, your role is to take responsibility first for yourself and your actions before you make the choice to change the world. Can you utilize your tools, be where you are, be you, and take responsibility?

There is a greater purpose. Use your tools because you are moving forward towards discovering your greater purpose. Your greater purpose is found in We-Consciousness. Can you shift your focus of attention to the greater purpose of the We? What is that greater purpose? What is the purpose of the We? What is the purpose of moving toward harmony, community, and equality? Where do you focus the majority of your attention? Are you making "what is" in your life your main focus? If so, can you shift your attention to the We for the fulfillment of the greater purpose of why you are here?

What is truly important to you? Is moving forward to build a new world of harmony, community, and equality important to you? Can you use the tools you have learned to continue to move through life with compassion and acceptance, and to focus on the We?

From your heart, what do you really want? Are you shifting your focus to the world that you say you want to live in? This is a choice. Questions that can guide you to live and embody your purpose are:

"Where am I?"

"What truly resonates in the depth of my heart?"

"What resonates for me 'out there' in the world?"

"Am I ready to serve the world?"

Epilogue
Living the Life You Say You Want, Living a Life You Love

By now you have come to realize that Michael's teachings are as surprisingly simple as they are powerful. Michael has given us a great gift by providing us with this set of tools to help us move through our lives. When these lessons were originally channeled through me, they came at two-week intervals over a span of forty weeks. For almost a year, I followed Michael's instructions to the letter, working on the lessons diligently, diving into each exercise for a full two weeks before the next arrived. I experienced profound and wonderful shifts in my life while processing the material at that pace.

Later, when the material was being transcribed and I began to arrange it into the form of a book, I worked through the lessons again—this time somewhat quicker—and, once again, I experienced a series of incredible shifts in my life. Michael's straightforward questions, especially "Where are you?" "What are you feeling?" and "What do you need?" helped me peel back layer after layer of armoring around my heart and to go deeper into my connection with myself, so I began to understand the truth of my being and genuinely love it.

With assurance, I can say that these lessons and the tools they contain are valuable to implement not once, but throughout a lifetime. In the preparation of this book, working alongside my friend Stephanie, for a third time I redid the lessons very slowly and deliberately, in order and in their entirety, and had a similar experience of being brought deeper into loving myself. The reason to do this work is to become open to receiving love.

If you're like me, you have to learn how to receive life and love. You have to learn how to open up until your heart is filled with love. Moving from your mind to living life from your heart is a process that doesn't happen in an instant, but by responding to life as it comes.

I am thoroughly convinced of the value of this material, which resonates in every fiber of my being, because my life has been transformed by having fully incorporated it into my lifestyle. My career has prospered, my relationships are genuine and meaningful, I feel more confident in every way, I am having more fun, and I love my life and the direction it is moving. It feels as if limitless possibilities are open to me and that I have found my path.

At no time have I ever become so stuck or frustrated with the process of feeling my feelings and identifying my needs that I wanted to throw this out the window. Not once. In fact, I now truly know the significance of exploring my feelings and getting at the root of any fear of lack and limitation, any sense of deprivation, any yearning and attachment that prevents me from moving forward. My commitment is to live my truth and be impeccable with my word, to grow and to learn—and to embrace this as my way of being. Now when life gets rocky, these tools and this approach are solid ground, my clear path to having the life I say I want. I love the man I see reflected in the mirror and giving to, and receiving love from him, as well as sharing that love with others.

Once you set the intention to do this work, your life will change on some level immediately. By doing this work you are essentially telling the universe that you are committed to having the life you want. If you are committed to living your soul's divine plan, it is important to know and live your truth, to live authentically with your heart wide open. Once you commit to a new way of being, one that is not based on conditioning from childhood, you will begin to create your life through resonance. As you walk the path, your relationships will reflect your commitments and who you are being. You will attract new people into your life who share the same resonance as yours, those who have a similar purpose in their lives. This is immensely fulfilling.

Michael's teachings can change your life. So be ready to take a good long look at your life today, and to keep on looking for the rest of your life. As you know by now, you will never finish this process. Do the exercises and move forward—generate some momentum—then look at what does and doesn't resonate. Come full circle back to the beginning of the process. Keep returning to Michael's questions, which will help you assess how to move forward from where you are in the moment. What do you need and what do you want? Everything you need to know will be shown to you if you can stay open in the face of not-knowing. The answers are already there, when you ask questions. Once your answers emerge, you always have new choices.

Can you be comfortable in not-knowing? Can you accept that your heart is being cracked wide open and love learning to be cracked open with a heart filled with love? You can choose to be in this place of wide open love and not know, even as you strongly desire to know. You can retrain your nervous system to be so open to the new that the unknown seems familiar.

The rewards of the journey you have undertaken come from within, not from the outer world. The aim is living a life you want, having what you want, being fulfilled by what you have, and enjoying yourself. Your life purpose is to live your truth, to be who you are and love yourself in every relationship and every situation. That is the way the world changes. You are part of the world; therefore your service to the world begins with your service to yourself. Everything follows from that. Who you are being matters, because you matter. The world needs you to come out of hiding, to drop disguises and your mask, and to really go for it—to go for being you in your greatest essence. When you transform how you are being, you transform the world.

One of the great beauties of this work is that it transforms the nature of relationships. The culmination of Michael's lessons is developing the natural ability to give and receive love and support. Thus, when you interact with others, it does not involve shaming or blaming. It involves acceptance and compassion, and supporting your brothers and sisters to live their highest good, which means helping them live their truths in the bigger picture of the divine plan.

Interestingly, our highest good and our purpose is that which brings us the most joy. If you can identify this, then you can state it clearly to another person. Support will come to you organically if you are clear in stating your needs and desires and are wide open to receive support. You will end up having more options than you can even imagine right now. Life will surprise you. For this reason, life typically accelerates when you do this work full on. Those who resonate with your purpose will be drawn to you organically. You will enter into relationships of a kind you never had before where you and others care about each other's highest good. This is the world of community, harmony, and equality about which Michael often speaks.

Just remember, this is not a competition. Your process will go at whatever speed it goes. Life is not a race. All that is required is to be where you are and to love yourself in your process. It's a little like pulling a cork out of a genie's bottle, except you are both doing the pulling and the genie. Once the bottle has been uncorked through doing the lessons and implementing the tools in this book, you are unleashed to create a life you love. By revealing your talents and gifts, you have discovered the path to your purpose. Your purpose will come into your life organically as soon as you pop the cork of your heart to receive that purpose.

What you thought you wanted when you began reading this book may not be what you have now, at the end of it—but I would guess that you love what you do have. If you are on this page, and you have done the twenty lessons in this book, you have certainly done the important work of at least beginning to define what love is for you. Your understanding of love will continue to deepen. Life has a divine order, its own natural timing, which is perfect. Simply let go of your agendas. You just need to be willing to show up and trust that you will be able to respond in the moment to what life offers. All you ever need do is to feel into your heart to assess if what is there is for your highest good. Life is flooding you with infinite possibilities and you are learning to navigate life by simply being in every moment.

Through doing this work, I have found that there are amazing opportunities for healing. In the mirror of our relationships we learn to see where our old patterns, habits, and rituals are being reflected, and also to recognize our value. Ongoing relationships are reassessed and long-ago connections are resolved. Loose ends are tied up. Some people drop away, even as others arrive. We are provided opportunities to give thanks, to offer apologies, and to honor others for having been in our lives as our teachers. Chances arise to let out what has been held within that kept us tied to the past. We have our feelings. We move forward towards the life we want.

Our conditioning would have us believe that we can't have the life we want for this, that, or another reason—and the reason is different for each of us. Our conditioning would have us believe that certain emotions and ways of being are not permissible, that they are shameful, dangerous, or wrong—and these emotions and ways of being are different for each of us. Our conditioning would have us believe that we cannot simultaneously give and receive. But these beliefs belong to the old way of life; they are not relevant in the new way of life.

If I had to name the shifts that have been monumental for me after practicing Michael's teachings, the first one that comes to mind is that I now focus on what is rather than on what is not. Also, I feel as if I have accessed the enthusiastic child inside me, the part that Michael has called the wonder child. I see the world as a magical place filled with possibilities. As a healed and individuated adult, the wounded child in me is no longer running my life. I am able to get things done, to consciously create my life, while playing at my life. And I no longer believe that every situation in my life is an either/or proposition. Nothing is exclusive.

So that is where I am.

Where are you?

About the Author

Jeff Fasano is a Reiki Master, Light Ascension Therapist, Trance Channel and a well respected photographer living in Los Angeles California. At the age of forty, he found his passion for photography and it has led him to living a life that he only imagined. This gift and passion has been the doorway for him to connect with his life purpose, and has led him to those who have made the same connection. He is channel and messenger for the energy and teachings of Archangel Michael. Imparting wisdom, guidance, and support, so we can love, honor and value who we are and find our passion to live our life's purpose. He is cofounder of the Angel News Network, the mission of which is to bring the messages of the divine realm into the earthly plane, thus contributing to humanity's spiritual growth and ascension by raising the consciousness, resonance, and vibration of the world.

Journey of the Awakened Heart is Jeff's first book. His earlier essay, "For the Love of It," was published in the anthology Audacious Creativity. You can see his photographic work at:

Jeff Fasano Photography
www.jefffasano.com
Learn more about his spiritual work at:

Jeff Fasano

Journey of the Awakened Heart
www.journeyoftheawakenedheart.net
The Angel News Network
www.theangelnewsnetwork.com

The Angel News Network Books

Coming Home to Lemuria:
An Ascension Adventure Story
by Phillip Collins

Life Mastery
by Joel Anastasi
with channel Jeff Fasano

The Second Coming
by Joel Anastasi
with channel Robert Baker

The Ascension Handbook
by Joel Anastasi
with channel Jessie Keener

Sacred Poetry & Mystical Messages
by Phillip Collins

Man Power God Power
by Phillip Collins

Happiness Handbook
by Phillip Collins

God's Glossary
By Phillip Collins

Activate Your Soul's Plan
By Phillip Collins

Learn more about The Angel News Network
and order these wonderful books at:
www.theangelnewsnetwork.com

Made in the USA
San Bernardino, CA
29 March 2015